Tàijíquán Wúwéi —

a Natural Process

Wee Kee-Jin

太極拳
無為

中正太極學院

TAIJI QUAN

SCHOOL OF CENTRAL EQUILIBRIUM

Published by
>   Taijiquan School of Central Equilibrium
>   PO Box 27-693
>   Mt Roskill
>   Auckland 1004
>   New Zealand

Cover and book design, layout and production: Dean Cudmore

Pīnyīn romanization: *Bouy-Lan Tan*

Photographs excepting those of *Huang Sheng-Shyan* : Dean Cudmore

Students photographed with *Wee Kee-Jin* performing *tuīshǒu* (pushing-hands)
in order of appearance: Marcus Henning, Hella Ebel, Dean Cudmore, Jimi Ooi

ISBN 0-473-09781-8

© Phil Mills

To my teacher *Huang Sheng-Shyan* for showing me the path,
to my students for accompanying me along the way,
and to my wife and sons for supporting me throughout my *tàijí* journey.

Contents

Part 1:

Introduction

Learning the art of *tàijí* was once exclusive to the *Chen* family and village members. However thanks to *Yang Lu-Chang* and subsequent generations, *tàijí* has extended throughout China and all over the world. Now there are five distinctive styles; *Chen, Yang, Wu, Sun* and *Hoa*, each named after their founding families. Further traditions derive from these, such as the *Cheng Man-ch'ing* approach to the *Yang* style.

Observers frequently assume that *tàijí* appears to be just a mobility exercise for the elderly Chinese. Certainly with its slow and soft movements, *tàijí* can be studied throughout a lifetime, but it is not exclusive to any age group, race or gender. Anyone can benefit from practising *tàijí* regularly.

Tàijí does not need special clothing, equipment or venue and isn't even dependant on the weather.

In today's world where so many things are fast or even instantaneous, *tàijí* stands out for its lessons in patience. The many subtle details mean that *tàijí* is not an easy art to learn and progress can't be rushed. Therefore the most essential requirement to studying *tàijí* is perseverance.

The emphasis is on relaxation and the letting go of unnecessary tension from the body. Constant refinement of this process results in an acute awareness of yourself, and later others.

Another common misconception is that *tàijí* is ineffective as a martial art. This is from the view that the strong conquer the weak and the fast beat the slow. However *tàijí* doesn't train you to overpower an opponent like other martial arts might. Instead you work on overcoming yourself (the ego) and operating in harmony with your opponent. *Tàijí* is more about maximising the efficiency and effectiveness of movements and minimising the effort and energy used to produce them. This eliminates any dependency on brute strength.

In the broader context *tàijí* is *Dào* (a philosophy) for living; the training to be a centred, balanced and harmonious human being in all situations, throughout life.

There are generally three reasons for learning *tàijí*; attaining and maintaining good health;

practising a martial art; and understanding the *Dào* (philosophy). Good health is the most valid because it is the foundation of human life, without your health you cannot accomplish anything else. The second most important reason would be for the purpose of understanding the *Dào*; *tàijí* can teach you how to be humane and co-exist with others and the universe. In this age of modern weapons, no matter how good or fast a martial artist you are, you will never be as quick as a bullet. If you are healthy and truly master the *Dào* of *tàijí*, there shouldn't be a need to fight.

Due to the growing popularity of *tàijí*, there are now a lot of videos and books available on the subject. However they can only serve as a reference and cannot replace a teacher. The *tàijí* "Song of the Thirteen Postures" classic clearly states; "To be shown the route to the [*tàijí*] door you need oral transmission".

The responsibility of maintaining the quality of the art, lies with both teacher and student.

"You go over thousands of mountains in search of a good teacher."

— *Huang Sheng-Shyan*

It is important not to base the criteria for your teacher choice, solely on their lineage. Not all students of good teachers reach a similar level. Choosing a teacher because he or she is a sibling or descendant of a famous practitioner is another unreliable basis, because *tàijí* is not genetically inherited. Another important point to remember is that a good teacher is not necessarily famous.

It is also a myth that all the good teachers are Chinese. I have personally come across a number of Westerners that have a better understanding of the *tàijí* principles than many Chinese teachers that I have encountered. *Huang Sheng-Shyan* often suggested to his students (nearly all Chinese), that if they did not practise seriously, one day they would have to learn *tàijí* in the west.

A good teacher is knowledgeable, with a deep understanding of the *tàijí* principles and importantly, the ability to apply them practically. He or she must be willing to impart their full knowledge to their students. A true teacher - student relationship only forms when the teacher begins to share their knowledge unreservedly.

Huang Sheng-Shyan
formally accepting
Wee Kee-Jin (author)
as an inner student

A good teacher must have the ability to fulfil the students' needs according to their level. A teacher must not just teach, he or she must continue to practise as this is the only way to raise the students' level. Teaching should be treated as just another phase of learning, however it is important to teach what the students should be practising, but train what you need to be working on yourself.

A teacher must avoid deviating from the principles and make *tàijí* into something mystical or fall into the trap of seeking guru worship. Both cases are getting carried away and losing touch with reality. The teacher must realise that the students are not commodities but rather training partners. When the students mature, the teacher must release them to pursue their own *tàijí* experiences and not to remain living in the teacher's shadow. A teacher is truly successful when the students surpass them. Teachers must remember that the students do not belong to them but are actually students of *tàijí*. Essentially both are simply colleagues helping each other along on the journey of *tàijí* .

"You go through tens of thousands of oceans in search of a dedicated student".

— *Huang Sheng-Shyan*

We must dispel the myth that only Chinese can reach the higher levels of *tàijí*. Sometimes understanding the Chinese language can actually be a handicap to learning *tàijí*; we may hear the principles spoken and take them at face value, but not look beyond the words into the deeper meaning.

Tàijí is not exclusive to any race, gender or age group. As long as you are human and have the patience, and perseverance to practise regularly, you can become good at *tàijí*.

Unfortunately most of today's students want to learn everything in a short space of time, and expect to become good without practising much. If a student decides to take up *tàijí* then he or she must be prepared to train regularly, otherwise it is of little benefit.

"Learning is eating, practising is digesting". Consistent practice is important for steady progress. Initially you must discipline yourself to practice, however later it needs to become enjoyable, so that you want to train.

Wee Kee-Jin (author) showing gratitude for being accepted as a student by Huang Sheng-Shyan

The student teacher relationship only develops if the student is willing to receive the knowledge that is being imparted. Students must have one hundred percent confidence in the teaching, and yet analyse what they learn. Doubts will only hinder progress.

As a student you need to have an open attitude, by being so you are receptive. If you constantly make comparisons to other teachers, you close yourself off.

You should regard any *tàijí* practitioner you meet as a teacher, that way you are always in a position to learn something from them. From someone whose standard is higher than yours, you can learn a deeper understanding of the principles. From someone whose standard is the same or lower than yours, you can learn to recognise not only their mistakes, but more importantly whether you are also making them.

Students must have an understanding of the *tàijí* principles to be able to analyse what they learn, so that they wont deviate from the *tàijí* path. To adhere to the principles, they must constantly analyse what they practise. No matter whom you learn from, you must always check that what you learn is in accordance with the principles contained in the 'classics'. Students must practise what is described in the 'classics' require not just what the teacher suggests, in case the teacher has strayed from the principles, or misunderstood them.

The students must be careful not to worship their teacher. It is important to remember that the teacher is only human. Worshipping, essentially means following blindly, without thinking.

There are different *tàijí* styles and many more forms, yet they are all only means to understanding the *tàijí* principles. To develop this understanding, students should choose one style with a form that they are comfortable with, and practise it diligently for a number of years. Learning many styles and forms may result in becoming a "Jack of all trades and master of none."

Since the reputed creation of *tàijíquán* by *Chang San-Feng*, many different styles and forms have evolved, each developed by their founders according to their understanding of the *tàijí* principles. Regardless of lineage the same theory applies.

Forms are only a means or tool, to understanding the principles. If you want to fly to London, England from Auckland, New Zealand, you could travel by different airlines, over different routes. Some will take a longer time, others shorter, but the important thing is to follow the principles of flight and stay airborne until you reach the destination.

When you reach the higher levels of *tàijí*, which style or form you train is unimportant. Any movement that you do, when in accordance with the principles, is *tàijí*. Your *tàijí* will no longer be confined to set physical movements, so that the form becomes formless, and your *tàijí* will be *dào*, a way of life.

Most *tàijí* practitioners assume that they have finished learning *tàijí* when they complete learning the form. *Huang Sheng-Shyan* once told me that, "when you have learned the movements of the whole *tàijí* form you have only discovered the pathway leading to the door of *tàijí*". Firstly walk that pathway by practising the external movements, then enter the hallway of *tàijí* by training the internal processes.

Tàijí is not simply a matter of moving from one posture to another. It is whether you understand the changes that create the movements. The essence of *tàijí* is to understand the changes during the transitions from one movement to another.

If one person is practising a single *tàijí* movement and adhering to the principles, yet another is performing whole forms without following the principles, then only the first one is actually doing *tàijí*. You might learn the movements of an entire form in a matter of a few years, however refining it is a life long process. We will always be students of *tàijí* and never masters of it.

To correctly practise a *tàijí* form, four conditions have to be present:

1. ***Jìn* (calmness):** - Quietening the mind and drawing your attention within, cultivates an acute awareness of the body. Once calm, you can use your awareness to listen to and observe how the body moves, while noting any tensions and instructing the body to relax.

2. ***Dìng* (stillness):** - Of both body and mind. There should not be any physical wavering and your thoughts should not drift off. Either will lead to the dispersion of *qì* (vital energy).

3. ***Sōng* (relaxation):** - Often *tàijí* practitioners misunderstand relaxed as being limp or floppy, that is however a lack of structure, and effectively collapsing. The Chinese word used in the classics that is translated as relax is *fàngsōng*, which literally means to "let go". To *fàngsōng* (relax) is to eliminate unnecessary tension from the body. Anything more than using the minimal amount of physical effort required to sustain the structure, produces tension. When you are relaxed, the parts of your structure are connected. When you are tense, the structure is disconnected. *Sōng* (relaxation) is produced by the cultivation of awareness, you must use awareness to create the relaxation in the body including during movement. What's more you can only *chén* (sink), when relaxed.

4. ***Chén* (sinking):** - There is both physical *chén* (sinking) and mental *chén* (sinking). Physical *chén* (sinking) refers to the dropping of the shoulders, softening of the torso and seating of the hips into the pelvic sockets. When you relax and drop the shoulder joints the arms connect with the body. When you relax and seat the *kuà* (hips) the body is connects to the base (the legs to the feet). Mental *chén* (sinking) is a process of letting the sensation of relaxation be guided by your mind's awareness, flowing down from the *níwán* (crown of the head) through the body, down the legs into the feet, passing through the *yǒngquán* (bubbling well)- the root, into the ground. This can also be referred to as the process of, "swallowing the *qì* of the heaven, connecting to the energy of the earth." It is from the *chén* (sinking) that the *jìn* (relaxed force) of *tàijí* is produced.

Shí and Xū

Shí (substantial / full) and *xū* (insubstantial / empty) are expressions of *yáng* and *yīn* respectively. These are not references to the distribution of body weight between the two feet. *Shí* and *xū* more closely represent the relationship between the forces. The fault of *shuāngzhòng* is often misinterpreted as being double weighted, but it actually translates as equal heaviness. Weight (*zhòngliàng*) is the effect of gravity on mass, therefore downwards. Heaviness is a pressure in any direction. So *shuāngzhòng* (equal heaviness) means opposing a *yáng* force with a *yáng* force.

The classics state, "when the left is *shí* (substantial), the left is *xū* (insubstantial), and when the right is *shí* (substantial) the right is *xū* (insubstantial)". This is the principle of cross-alignment in which the force from the left foot should be issued through the right arm and the force from the right foot should be issued through the left arm. The error of *shuāngzhòng* (equal heaviness) is most obvious when the force of left foot is issued through the left arm, or the force right hand transfers the force from the right foot. In addition when an opponent's force arrives, and you resist at the point of contact, it is also *shuāngzhòng* (equal heaviness), *yáng* against *yáng*.

Ultimately in every part of the body there is both *shí* (substantial) and *xū* (insubstantial), it is constantly changing in relation to circumstances.

Many *tàijí* practitioners consider equally distributing the body weight over both feet (50/50) as being *shuāngzhòng*. However if this were the case, the very beginning posture of the form would be wrong.

The Human level focuses on the physical structure of the movement, the physical connection of the movement and the sequence of changes that create the physical movement.

To lay the foundation for the earth level, the physical movements of the *tàijí* form have to be accurate and executed naturally. For someone who practises consistently every day, this would normally take about three years to achieve.

Wang Ts'ung – Yueh's classic states: "To miss by a fraction of a *lí* is to miss by a thousand *lí*". It highlights the importance of accuracy throughout the *tàijí* form, both when in position and during the transitions.

The need for precision was again emphasised by *Wang Ts'ung-Yueh* when he wrote, "It [the movement] must not fall short and it must not be overdone". Any inaccuracy caused by overdoing or under doing a movement, will result in the misalignment of the body posture which becomes either locked up, or exposed to an attack. These bad habits will also transfer into the *tuīshǒu* (pushing-hands), as the way you move in the form will be the same way you move while pushing-hands.

"Understand yourself and understand your opponent, [then] you will excel in *tuīshǒu* (pushing-hands)." Understanding yourself develops through learning to synchronise your body movements in the *tàijí* manner, first learnt during the form, where there isn't an external force affecting you.

The *tàijí* form is the substance, and the *tuīshǒu* (pushing-hands) are the applications. The substance must be properly structured before we can consider the applications.

The physical movements of the form relate to three specific regions, the base, the upper body and the arms. None of which are ever entirely straightened in any *tàijí* structure, including the upper body, which although upright is not held rigid. All joints from the ankles, knees, hips, spine, shoulders, elbows and wrists must remain free and unlocked, so that the body is always mobile.

1.   The Base (feet, legs and hips)

The base movement refers to any movement from the feet through to the *kuà* (hips), and represents the foundation of the structure in the *tàijí* form. If the foundation is neglected, the structure will collapse, just as in the construction of a tall building.

There is a saying concerning Chinese martial arts: "If you practise [a martial art] without paying attention to your *gōng* (base) then it will be a lifetime of empty practice." *Huang Sheng-Shyan* would emphasise this point by repeating the following story:

A teacher once told a student, that he should leave as he had received the full martial arts knowledge, however he was to visit every year and have his progress checked. The first year, he came bringing gifts for the teacher, and demonstrated in front of him. The teacher made the comment; "You do not have xiá gōngfū". The second year the student returned, again with gifts for the teacher, and following his practise the teacher repeated the criticism, "You still do not have xiá gōngfū". The third year the student came with a gift, but as the teacher was out he was instead met by his wife. Being a proficient martial artist herself, she suggested that the student practice in front of her. After seeing how diligent the student was, she explained to him that not having xiá gōngfū had two meanings, one was not practising enough, the other was not paying attention to his base work. She went on to clarify that it was the second fault that her husband had observed. When the teacher later came home and saw the gifts, he enquired about the student. His wife answered that he had already left and that she had told him the real meaning of xiá gōngfū. The teacher sighed and told his wife not to expect any more gifts from the student, as now that he knew the secret, he would not need to return.

i.   **The Feet:**

The feet provide the 'root', it is through them that the body structure connects into the earth. This is termed 'grounding'. Whether receiving or discharging a force, the feet must be firmly grounded. At all times the feet should feel as though settled into sand or semi-set concrete. The body weight should be evenly distributed over the whole sole of the foot, with the toes relaxed. Gripping the toes causes the *yǒngquán* (bubbling well) to disconnect from the ground. The classics point-out that, "when the *yǒngquán* (bubbling well) has no root, the *yāo* (waist) has no control".

ii.   **The Ankles and Knee Joints:**

The ankles joint should always remain relaxed and loose. The front knee vertically aligns with the big toe of the front foot, so that the sole can remain in full contact with the ground. In the bow (archer) stance, the back knee stays in line with the big toe of the back foot. Any inward collapsing of the back knee will result in the disconnection of the outside of back foot from the ground, and the restriction of the rear *kuàgēn* (hip joint).

The back leg doesn't straighten when sitting back in the *tàijí* form, so the rear knee should remain at the same height. Lengthening the back leg while sitting back, is effectively standing up, which decreases the connection of the back foot from the ground. The backward movement is eased by the front knee 'giving', if the front knee locks, there can only be a downward but no backward movement.

When moving forward, the back knee should drop down towards the foot, by relaxing the foot and 'letting go' at the ankle joint. This creates a spring like compression in the rear leg. Be careful not to force the knee down by simply bending the back leg, as poor alignment or over bending, can cause injury to the knee. To avoid this, ensure that the entire back foot remains in full contact with the ground throughout the forward movement, therefore the back knee must stay in line with the toes, and not collapse inwards.

Demonstration of:
Knee not forward
enough

Demonstration of:
Correct knee
position

Demonstration of:
Knee too far
forwards

Demonstration of:
Knee collapsed inwards

Demonstration of:
Correct knee position

Demonstration of:
Knee pushed outwards

iii. *Kuàgēn* (hip joints):

The *kuàgēn* (hip joints) are where the body torso connects to the base. Many *tàijí* practitioners relax their *kuà* (hip area) but neglect to 'seat' the joints. If the *kuàgēn* (hip joints) aren't seated, the body cannot connect into the base. This results in the incoming forces jamming at the hips, and any energy that is borrowed from the earth, being unable to pass from base into the body, therefore becoming unavailable for the arms and hands.

Seating the hips begins at the moment of 'letting go' (relaxing) from the base. The area around the *kuàgēn* (hip joints) must immediately soften to provide the freedom for the ball of the femur to settle deep into the pelvic socket. Throughout all *tàijí* practices, both hips joints should be relaxed and seated. While in transition from one posture to another during the form, the body will tilt to the side if both *kuàgēn* (hip joints) don't seat at the same time. If either of your *kuàgēn* (hip joints) pop up during *tuīshǒu* (pushing-hands), you disconnect yourself from your base and then you are easily uprooted.

Demonstration of:
Rear hip not seated therefore tilting body

Demonstration of:
Front hip not seated therefore tilting body

Demonstration of:

Hips relaxed and seated evenly

In the releasing/issuing of the force during both the *tàijí* form and *tuīshǒu* (pushing-hands), the *kuàgēn* (hip joints) should remain seated and relaxed. Any outward or upward movement of the hips will result in the body leaning, the loss of the centre of equilibrium or the disconnection of the body from the base. All of which disrupt the flow of the force.

Often the statement in the classics of the '*yāo* initiating the turning', is misunderstood as being the waist on its own. However turning the waist without the hips, twists the body. It is the *kuà* (hips) together with the *yāo* (waist), which initiates all turning.

2.   **The Upper Body** (the crown of the head to the tail bone):

The first principles relating to the body are to tuck under the *wěilǘ* (tail bone) and draw in the chin. By maintaining these adjustments, keeping a light consciousness on the crown of the head and visualising the body to be suspended from above, the *níwán* and the *huìyīn* meridian points align. This allows the *qì* to flow freely through the three gates (*wěilǘ, yùzhěn* and *níwán*).

An imaginary line from the *níwán* to the *huìyīn* represents the body's central axis. By keeping this vertical, the body structure is described as being in a state of *zhōngzhèng* (central equilibrium).

In the original thirteen *tàijí* postures, the centre is represented by the "earth" element. Being centred means maintaining the state of *zhōngzhèng* (central equilibrium), which is the foundation for the other twelve postures. When *zhōngzhèng* (central equilibrium) is achieved, the feet are balanced and grounded, and the body is able to absorb forces from any direction. Therefore the body should be upright, relaxed and agile in every movement, so that it can change left and right, up and down, forwards and backwards or in any combination.

The body muscles must be released from tension. Unnecessary tension in the muscles will obstruct the force coming from the base into the arms, and prevent the *qì* from sinking into the *dāntián*. The classics state that during *fājìn* (issuing of force) the body must be totally *sōng* (relaxed) and *chén* (sunk). If the body tenses, the opponent's force will have something to utilise.

In every movement in the *tàijí* form, waves of relaxation must pass downwards through the body muscles, by using mind awareness to visualise the body as 'melting'. This will connect the base through to the arms. If the body muscles are tense, then the base and arms movements may co-ordinate, but wont connect. Meaning they may be moving at the same time, but will be independent of each other. The classic says, "when one part of the body moves, every part moves along with it. When one part arrives, every part arrives". In other words the whole movement of the body is one part leading another, and the speed of each keeping relative to the changes of the other. The destination is different but the time of arrival is the same.

To "*hán* (contain - not reveal) the chest and *bá* (spread) the back" is misunderstood by some *tàijí* practitioners, as concaving their chests and hunching their backs. This can be prevented by maintaining the central equilibrium, remaining conscious of the crown of the head, and visualising the body to be suspended from above. Then by softening the chest from within, the shoulder blades will naturally drop downwards instead of being pulled forwards. When the principle of "*hán* (contain - not reveal) the chest and *bá* (spread) the back" is correctly observed, the *qì* is able to sink into the *dāntián*.

The head should be lightly held with the chin gently drawn in, being careful to avoid tension developing in the neck. The tip of the tongue is lightly placed on the roof of the mouth, just behind the front teeth, so that saliva secretes and moistens the mouth. The eyes gaze unfocussed on a horizontal line (you see but you don't look), and sounds hardly register (you hear but are not listening). The attention remains on the internal changes, so that the *shén* (spirit) is kept within.

3.   Arms (shoulders, elbows, wrist, palms):

The *tàijí* principles state "*sōng* (relax) the shoulders, drop the elbows" and also "*chén* (sink) the shoulders, drop the elbows". Many *tàijí* practitioners work on relaxing their shoulders but neglect to sink them. The shoulders connect the arms to the body so by not sinking them, the arms become disconnected and the *qì* is prevented from sinking into the *dāntián*.

To *chén* (sink) the shoulders they must first *sōng* (relax), and at the same time soften the area around the joints so that the shoulder blades have a downward motion.

The dropping of the elbows is directly related to the relaxation and sinking of the shoulders. When the shoulders lift, the elbows lift and visa versa. To drop the elbows, allow the arms to hang by their own weight, taking care however, not to collapse them. If the elbow falls within the distance of a fist width from the torso, the arm has collapsed. In the *tuīshǒu* (pushing-hands) and the *fājìn* (releasing/issuing) the dropping of the elbows is used to break the opponent's root, by pivoting or spiralling the force into his or her base.

The hands are held open with the fingers relaxed. The fingers should not be completely straightened nor curved in (clawed), neither held tightly together nor stretched apart. The only exceptions to this are the closed palm positions used in the punches and planting of the fist, but even in these cases the fingers are relaxed, not clenched.

Whenever the hands are by the side of the body, the wrists are relaxed and seated with the fingers pointed diagonally downwards.

Demonstration of:
Beautiful lady's hand
side view

Demonstration of:
Beautiful lady's hand
front view

When a palm is in front of the body facing outwards, the wrist is unbent to produce the "beautiful lady's hand". The fingers are not quite straightened and just in contact with each other. The tip of the thumb should be in line with the central axis of the body, and the arc between the thumb and index fingers, at shoulder height. This is evident in postures such as *àn* (push), *dān biān* (single-whip), *lǒu xī* (brush-knee) and *niǎn hóu* (repulse monkey).

The Physical Movements in *Tàijí* Forms:

According to Chang Sang Feng's *tàijí* classic, "throughout all movements, the body should be light, agile and most importantly connected together".

In every movement in the *tàijí* form, the body, arms and base should be connected and completely relaxed, free of tension, and the central equilibrium maintained, as well as the feet firmly rooted. This applies throughout the movements, in transition and during the *fājìn* (releasing the force).

Before you can release the force (an upwards movement) in any posture, you must first sink (a downwards movement). This provides the connection for "borrowing the energy of the earth".

The space for the downward sinking is actually created from the ground up. Firstly by relaxing the feet, which connects the *yǒngquán* (bubbling well) to the ground, then giving at the joints: ankles, knees, and *kuà* (hips), to connect the body into the base. Followed by the letting go of the body, sinking of the shoulders and dropping of the elbows, for the arms to connect with the body.

The upward movement in *tàijí* is produced by the release of the compression developed from the sinking. This release or *fājìn* initiates in the feet, and becomes magnified in the legs. At this moment the tail bone tucks under, while the *kuà* (hips) seat, thus keeping the body in connection with the base. Waves of relaxation should ripple through the body muscles and then, because of the relaxing and sinking of the shoulders connecting the arms with the body, the arms will extend slightly. Dropping the elbows and maintaining the beautiful lady's wrist, transfers the force that originated at the feet, into the palms and fingers.

According to the principle, "from the feet through the legs, through the body to the fingers is one continuous flow of *qì*", it is necessary to have a smooth, uninterrupted flow of movement.

Sitting back, moving forward, stepping back and stepping forward, are all initiated by the base, the upper body does not lead. Similar to a motorcycle that transports the rider forwards, it is the base that moves the upper body to and fro.

Whether stepping, moving forwards and backwards, turning in transition, sinking into position, or releasing the force, the upper body should always be upright. This is possible providing the *kuà* (hips) are seated, the *wěilǘ* (tail bone) is tucked in, and a consciousness remains on the *níwán* (crown of the head), while visualising being suspended from above.

Forward Movements:

When in the bow stance, the feet are a shoulder width apart, the outside of the front sole points straight ahead, and the back foot is rotated inwards forty-five degrees. For diagonal postures such as *yù nǚ chuān suō* (fair lady weaves her shuttles), both heels are in line and the back foot is rotated 15° inwards.

When moving forward from either position, the body should travel directly along the centre line. Shifting to one side is a common mistake made by many *tàijí* practitioners.

To move forwards the pairs of ankles, knees and hips must "let go" at the same time and continue to relax at the same rate. The *kuàgen* (hip joints) drop vertically and the tail bone should tuck under, so that both a downward and forward movement is generated, pushing the front knee away. This same action connects both feet to the ground and creates compression in the rear leg. It is important that throughout the transfer the back knee remains in line with the toes of the back foot. The forward movement is complete when the front knee aligns directly above the front toes, and this represents the optimum moment to *fājìn* (release the relaxed force).

Far page top
demonstration of:
Shifting from one side to other
while moving forwards

Far page bottom
demonstration of:
Correctly moving forwards
along the centre line

This page
demonstration of:
Sitting back correctly, remaining upright
and moving away from the arms

Backward Movements:

Similar to moving forwards, sitting back tracks along the centre line. The backward movement is initiated by seating and drawing back both hip joints simultaneously, synchronised with the relaxation of both ankles and both knees. This ensures that the body remains upright. If the backward movement is produced by pushing back from the front foot, or pulling back the buttocks, the upper body is very likely to lean. Care should also be taken not to push up the back knee or jam the hips while sitting back, either of which will decrease the connection of the back foot with the ground. Failing to relax the front knee when moving backwards, results in a degree of standing up rather than the required small downwards movement.

Stepping Forwards:

At the transition point, just before stepping into the bow stance, the body faces a corner. To be able to step without lurching, the body weight must be entirely in the back (substantial) foot, with both hips relaxed and seated. Any holding on to either the substantial or insubstantial hip, will cause the body to tilt sideways.

The stepping of the front (empty) foot forwards is synchronised with the mind awareness sinking into the back (substantial) foot. This prevents the hips from coming up and ensures the grounding and stability are maintained during the transition. When the heel of the front (insubstantial) foot touches the ground, both hips joints must drop vertically downward to create the forward movement in the front (insubstantial) knee. The moment the front toes touch the floor, the

Far page - demonstration of:
Incorrectly sitting back by pulling from the buttocks

This page - demonstration of:
Stepping forwards with the toes touching too soon and rocking forwards

front knee should be vertically aligned with the toes. At this point the body will be in the central position, still facing the corner, and the weight distributed fifty-fifty.

The back foot then pivots on the heel so that the toes turn in forty-five degrees (or fifteen degrees if both heels are in line for the diagonal postures).

To square up to the final direction of the posture, the hips drop downward, and the back knee gives so that the leg bends and compresses into the back foot. Meanwhile the front knee is kept directly above the front toes. The back knee must stay aligned to the back toes, so that the back foot can be kept in full contact with the ground and the substantial hip kept open. When squaring up, ensure that the base and body turn around the central axis, taking care not to push either forwards or sideways. At the moment of *fājìn* (releasing) the weight distribution should be fifty-five percent on the back foot and forty-five percent in the front.

At an advanced stage, the squaring up combines with the adjustment of the back foot.

Stepping Backwards:

When stepping backwards for postures such as *niǎn hóu* (repulse monkey), *tuì bù kuā hǔ* (step-back to ride the tiger) and the transition before *yòu fēn jiǎo* (separate right leg), the physical weight transfer is synchronised with a continuous sinking of the mind awareness into the substantial foot. The hips remain relaxed and seated at all times to provide the stability and grounding during the transition. Care should be taken to keep the body upright while the foot is moving backwards. The toes must touch the ground first, immediately followed by the simultaneous relaxation of both ankles, knees and hip joints. This produces and combines the backward movement of the

Far page - demonstration of:
Stepping forwards correctly with the toes and knee arriving simultaneously, followed by adjusting the back foot 45°

This page - demonstration of:
Stepping backwards while remaining upright

Far page - demonstration of:

Stepping back correctly with the weight transfer synchronised with the body movement

This page - demonstration of:

Unsynchronised backwards stepping with heel contacting ground before weight transfer is complete

upper body, with the weight transfer into the back foot, and enables the body to remain vertical throughout. Both the physical movement and the weight transfer should be completed at the exact moment the back heel touches the ground.

Lifting of leg for kicking:

When executing a kick, the weight bearing leg must stay bent at the knee, and the hip seated. Any straightening of the leg, pushing up of the hip joint or tipping of the pelvis, will result in instability and loss of grounding.

Demonstration of:
Sweeping lotus kick with weight
bearing leg bent, and hips seated

General Body Movement:

The body is connected to the base by the relaxation and seating of the hips. Both the forward and backward movements of the body, are initiated by the base (legs).

To maintain *zhōngzhèng* (central equilibrium) the body must remain upright (as detailed in the previous chapter) throughout the transitions, when in position and during the *fājìn* (release).

Turning the Body:

There are basically two principles that guide the turning of the body.

1. Turning is initiated by the *kuà* (hip joints) and the *yāo* (waist): Many *tàijí* books suggest turning solely from the waist. However if you turn from the waist without turning the hips, the body will twist. The correct method is to turn from the *kuà* (hip joints) and rotate the waist, which orientates the body and directs the arms.

2. The millstone turns but the axle does not [turn]: Visualise the body as a millstone. Imagine a line running from the *níwán* (crown of the head) through the body connecting to the *huìyīn* meridian point. This line will serves as an axle (axis) within the body. When turning, visualise the body rotating around the axle.

When these two principles are observed, the body can turn left or right, yet remain upright and level, with the centre of equilibrium maintained.

Demonstration of:

Turning correctly from the hips, with the body, head and arms moving as one

Demonstration of:
Turning incorrectly from the shoulders,
with the head not following the movement,
causing the upper body to twist

Movement of Arms:

"Moving the arms is not *tàijí*", *Cheng Man-ch'ing* often quoted *Yang Cheng-Fu* and *Yang Pan Hou*. This does not mean that your arms do not move during *tàijí*, rather the arms do not move independently.

My teacher *Huang Sheng-Shyan* often said, "If there is no initiation of movement by the base, there should be no movement of the arms".

Any upward movement of the arms originates from the feet, magnifies through the legs, ripples through the body and is expressed through the fingers by the relaxation and sinking of the shoulders and dropping of the elbows.

Downward movements of the arms begin with the relaxation the feet, which creates the space for the ankles, knee and hip joints to relax and sink into. This is closely followed by the melting of the body muscles and sinking of the shoulders. Finally drop the elbows and seat the wrists.

Left, right or circular movement of the arms are all initiated by the turning of the hips, waist and body, all synchronised while relaxing and sinking the shoulders, and dropping of the elbows.

For the arm and body movements to be connected and not just coordinated, whenever the arms moves, the shoulders must relax and sink. To connect the body with the base, the *kuà* (hips) must be seated and a wave of relaxation needs to ripple downwards through the trunk of the body.

The movement during the *fājìn* from the bow stance postures:

During the *fājìn* from a bow stance with the left foot at the rear, the left leg only extends slightly. Throughout the release, the left knee stays in line with the left toes, so the left *kuà* (hip) must remain seated and open, but not pushed out.

Meanwhile the right knee remains in line with the front toes. The right hip stays relaxed and seated so that as the left foot's force is released through to the right arm, the force becomes stored in the right foot. Once the original release has been completed, by continuing to sink, another wave rebounds from the right foot through the left arm/hand. If the front hip is pushed out during the *fājìn* from the back foot, no sinking will take place into the front foot so the circle of force will be broken.

When the right foot is at the back and the left is in the front, the process is the mirror of the description above.

During the *fājìn* the upper body must relax, the chest soften, the shoulders sink and the elbows drop. The dropping of the elbows pivots (spirals) the force into the base of the opponent and breaks the root.

Any tensing of the body muscles obstructs the force as it passes through that area. Any lifting of the shoulders disconnects the arms from the body, resulting in the force from the base being unable to transfer into the arms through to the fingertips.

This page - demonstration of:
Refined fājìn produced by the rear leg only straightening a maximum of 5cm, and the shoulders dropping to send the arms out

Far page - demonstration of:
Unrefined pushing, produced by over extending the back leg which causes the body to lean forwards

The physical process of *fājìn* (releasing) does not require any further weight transfer to the front. In other words, no propelling yourself forwards by driving the from the back leg. Pushing the body downward is also unnecessary.

The movement during the *fājìn* from the single foot postures

The release of the relaxed force in the postures such as: *tí shǒu* (raise hands), *lǚ* (roll-back), *shǒu huī pí pá* (play guitar) and *niǎn hóu* (repulse monkey), is produced by *chén* (sinking) the mind awareness into the foot that is in full contact with the ground. The leg of the substantial foot must remain slightly bent (not straightened) and both hips need to be relaxed and seated. As in all the *fājìn*, the upper body must be upright and relaxed, the shoulders sunk and the elbows dropped.

Breathing:

One of the first things I directly asked *Huang Sheng-Shyan* about, was regarding the breathing. His reply was, "Let it be natural, don't force it". On other occasions he said that, "If you are relaxed and calm, you should not even be able to hear the sound of your own breathing".

We are all born with the natural ability to breathe, so there is no need to learn when to inhale or exhale.

In *tàijí* the long and thin breathing down to the *dāntián* happens naturally when you are truly relaxed. When you have a conversation we do not think of which word to breathe in and which word to breathe out. If you have to think of breathing then it is not natural.

Perhaps the reason for the modern *tàijí* fixation on the breath, comes from the misinterpretation of *qì*, which originally meant "rising steam". From that, two common meanings have emerged for the same Chinese character (氣): breath and energy. In the context that it is used throughout the classics, *qì* should be translated as energy.

To my knowledge there is only one direct reference to breathing in the classics, "Only with the ability to inhale and exhale, will there be agility" (from the Understanding the Thirteen Postures).

At the time of writing the classics, the character (呼) for *hū* would have been more likely to be used to refer to breathing.

The mind:

In *tàijí* we need to distinguish between certain functions of the mind: *yì* (intention), *tīng* (awareness) and *xīn* (conscience), as well as the difference between conscious and the subconscious states.

Before actually doing any action, there is first *yì* (an intention) to do it. For example, to go the toilet, you first think of it, followed by going there. You do not go there first, then later have the urge to go. Similarly in *tàijí* before you begin any movement you must first have an intention, which motivates the movement. The *yì* must be followed by *tīng*, a conscious awareness of actually doing the movement. The *yì* (intention) is the "planning" and *tīng* (awareness) is paying attention to the "doing". In *tàijí* an intention without awareness is known as *sǐ yì* (dead mind), a mind without life.

It is through the conscious mind that we gain an understanding of the changes that create the movements. The circulation of *qì* is cultivated by the conscious mind. When the mind awareness travels, the *qì* flows. The relaxation of the body is also cultivated by the conscious mind, using the awareness of the body to let go the tension in the body.

The subconscious mind is a later development of using the conscious mind. In the beginning you use the conscious mind to move and synchronise the changes to create the *tàijí* movement, to circulate the *qì* in the movement, to guide the relaxation, to note the connections and whether you are centred. After prolonged practice everything becomes natural, so you will no longer need to be conscious of everything that is happening. What should take place, happens without you having to be aware of it. At this very advanced stage, movements become spontaneous. This is time when the subconscious mind has taken over from the conscious mind.

When first learning *tàijí* you are unlikely to have a clear *yì* (intention) or much *tīng* (awareness) of your movements. To progress, you need to cultivate both the intention and awareness of all your movements. Until the movements become second nature (subconscious) yet perfectly precise, then you will no longer require a conscious intention or awareness.

Developing *xīn* (conscience) is perhaps the highest level of the mental stage of *tàijí*. One of the first things that *Huang Sheng-Shyan* told me was that, "My progress in *tàijí* would depend on how I am as a human being". At the time I was very sceptical of this statement, however later on my *tàijí* journey, I began to see the truth in it.

It became evident that it was necessary overcome the ego, particularly pride, selfishness, jealousy, and more subtly, the desire to dominate over others. If we can overcome these obstacles, our *xīn* (conscience) becomes clear and our *qì* harmonises.

Then we can truly relax and be in harmony with ourselves, with others, with society and the universe. Not only will we be able to discover the centre of equilibrium within the body but more importantly, the centre of equilibrium within the mind. This is how the body and mind become one, achieving action without action. Just as the *Wang Ts'ung-Yueh* classic advises, "…forget oneself, and follow the other". Follow the *xīn* (heart / conscience) and *yì* (mind).

Spiritual development in *tàijí* is not waiting for some mysterious entity to enter you and provide enlightenment, it is harmonising with everyone and everything around you. By accomplishing this, and letting everything be natural, you will be living the *tàijí* principles rather than just physically practising *tàijí*. Then the form will have become formless.

The earth level of *tàijí* cultivates the flow of *qì* (energy) in the body while executing the movements in the *tàijí* form. When practising on the earth level, the principles of the human level must be continued to maintain the structure and alignment for the *qì* to circulate.

Qì is the life energy that naturally flows throughout our body. Although the Chinese character is written in the same way, it differs from the *qì* that we breathe.

The 'Understanding the Thirteen Postures' classic states that, "The *yì* (mind intention) motivates the *qì*", and also, "The *qì* motivates the body". Therefore the flow of the *qì* is motivated using intention and conscious mind awareness.

To achieve this, you must first gather the *shén* (spirit) within, which requires focusing the attention inside the body, freeing the mind of other thoughts and preventing the mind from wandering off. Then you will enter a state of meditation in motion.

Next there needs to be an intention to circulate the *qì*, so that it can flow through the body, by moving the mind awareness. If there is only an intention but no awareness, the *qì* can stagnate. However if the mind intention or awareness is too intense, it will lead back to stiffness.

The first stage of the Earth level is to gather the *qì* into the *dāntián*, which is located about 5 centimetres below the navel, and in terms of depth, two thirds closer to the navel than to the spine. The *dāntián* is also known as, "the sea of the *qì*".

To be able to sink the *qì* into the *dāntián*, the physical body must be relaxed, upright and totally connected, with the *wěilǚ* (tail bone) tucked in. At this stage, when practising every movement of the form, the practitioner must send a wave of flowing *tīng* (mind awareness) from the *níwán* (crown of the head), through the body into the legs and feet. When the *tīng* (mind awareness) passes through the trunk of the body, keep a light consciousness at the *dāntián* for a few seconds. This is to gather the *qì* into the *dāntián* and must only be done using a light consciousness, not using any force or over concentration.

Once the *qì* is gathered in the *dāntián,* it can be dispersed to other parts of the body. Being able to send it down through the legs into the feet, through the *yǒngquán* (bubbling well) and into the ground, is the beginning of the second stage of the Earth level, and is an internal process in *tàijí* known as *chén* (sinking). It is through this process that the practitioner connects with the earth "to borrow its energy", which produces *jìn* (relaxed *tàijí* force). Without *chén* (internally sinking), no *jìn* can be generated.

The first time this is taught is when moving into every posture position, prior to the releasing of force. For example once in the bow stance for postures such as *péng* (ward-off), *jǐ* (press), or *àn* (push), send a wave of mind awareness from the *níwán* (crown of the head) flowing down through the body, *dāntián*, legs into both feet, through the *yǒngquán* (bubbling well), deep into the ground beneath both feet. As a result, there should be a noticeable increase in pressure of both feet against the floor, which we term, 'grounding'.

Similarly in postures where the weight is only on a single foot (i.e. when only one foot is in contact with the ground), the wave of awareness extends deep into the ground through the substantial foot. Again there should be an increase in grounding of that foot.

Once the sinking of the *qì* into the ground is experienced clearly in posture, it can be practised during the transitions in the form. When sitting back, send a wave of mind awareness from the *níwán* down the body, into the back leg, through the *yǒngquán* (bubbling well) of the back foot deep into the ground. When moving forward, send a wave of mind awareness from the *níwán*, down the body, through the legs, into the feet and project it deep into the ground beneath both feet. When stepping forwards or backwards, send the mind awareness into the ground under the foot that is in contact with the ground. Eventually the sinking process is included both during the transitions and when in position, with overlapping waves of mind awareness sinking into the ground from the transition through to being in position.

When first working on sinking the *qì*, the continuity of the physical movements of the form is not as important. The focus is on the mind awareness sinking into the ground under the feet, being completed before moving on to the next posture.

The third stage of the Earth level is to draw the *qì* back from the ground to the fingertips. This is also the process referred to as "borrowing the energy from the earth". *Huang Sheng-Shyan* always emphasised that when you *chén* (internally sink), you always send the *qì* into the ground and when you draw up the *qì*, you always extend it to the fingertips.

Once you complete sinking the *qì* into the feet and ground in any *tàijí* posture, you visualise it rebounding from the ground back through the *yǒngquán* (bubbling well) of the feet, up the legs, through the body, shoulders, arms and into the fingertips.

While this is happening, the feet must remain firmly connected to the ground and the body must stay upright with the centre of equilibrium maintained. The *kuà* (hip joints) must also be seated, the trunk of the body relaxed, the chest softened from within, the shoulders sunk, elbows dropped and palms and fingers relaxed. If any of these are not maintained, it will break the flow of *qì* and prevent it from reaching the fingertips.

The theory of 'cross-alignment' requires that the *qì* from the left foot, flows through to the right fingertips, and the *qì* from the right foot flows through to the left fingertips. This is supported by

Wang Ts'ung – Yueh's tàijí classic which states, "When the left is substantial, the left is insubstantial, and when the right is substantial, the right is insubstantial".

The final stage of the earth level is to moving the *qì* from the *dāntián*, through the *huìyīn* meridian point into the three gates; *wěilú, yùzhěn* and *níwán (bǎihùi)*, thereby connecting the *ren (front mid-line)* and *du (back mid-line)* meridians. After prolonged gathering of the *qì* in the *dāntián* the *qì* will naturally flow through the *huìyīn* into these three gates.

It is still crucial to keep the body upright with the tail bone tucked under, the chin drawn in and consciousness on the crown of the head. When I was practising the form, *Huang Sheng-Shyan* would often put an empty matchbox on the crown of my head, for the specific purpose of raising the *shén* (spirit).

Eventually, when the process at the earth level becomes completely natural, it is no longer necessary for a conscious intention or mind awareness to circulate the *qì*. At this stage the *qì* will circulate subconsciously so that "the *qì* is constantly in every part of the body".

The cultivation of sensitivity and feelings of a partner through *tuīshǒu* (pushing-hands) is the purpose of the Heaven level. Training the ability to listen to (sense) external forces, and developing an understanding of the incoming forces and your own body's response to them.

The Heaven develops three qualities:- *tīngjìn* (listening energy), *dǒngjìn* (understanding energy) and *shénmíng* (spiritual clarity).

1.   *Tīngjìn* (listening energy):

To be able to "listen" to the forces, there must be contact between you and your training partner, which includes all of the elements of sticking/adhering, connecting, not resisting and not disconnecting.

Nián: - To adhere; to stay in contact or stick to the force at all times. It is necessary both in attacking and withdrawing, whether you are advancing or yielding/neutralising.

Lián: - To connect to your partner's centre/root, both during and after neutralising his or her attack. When a forward force lands on you, yield and neutralise, remaining in contact. When your partner withdraws, you follow without losing contact to his or her centre. In both cases you connect behind your opponent's force, and are in a position to counter attack.

Not resisting nor disconnecting: - if a force advances a centimetre, and you only withdraw half a centimetre, you are resisting. When a force advances a centimetre, and you pull away by one and the half centimetres, you are disconnecting. It is also disconnecting if the opponent withdraws a centimetre, and you only follow by half a centimetre.

Nián (sticking), *lián* (connecting), not-resisting and not-disconnecting are all interrelated. To develop them, and therefore cultivate *tīngjìn*, you must respond like a sponge, which only moves as much as the force that is exerted against it, and follows back only as far as the force that is being released determines.

2.   *Dǒngjìn* (understanding energy):

Actually a refined form of *tīngjìn*. You can only understand the force after you have 'heard' it.

The classic 'Understanding the Thirteen Postures' says, "If the other [person] does not move, I do not move. If the other [person] has the slightest movement, I move ahead". This requires *dǒngjìn*, and suggests that the timing and extent of all movements are under your control.

To acquire *dǒngjìn* you need to learn to distinguish between an attacking and withdrawing force, to recognise both the direction of the incoming force and where to lead it, and to differentiate substantiality and insubstantiality, not just within yourself, but also within your partner.

First differentiate basic substantiality from insubstantiality, comparing what is left from right, up from down, within yourself and then within your opponent. Ultimately you should be able to detect the substantial from the insubstantial within the space of a fingertip.

Yielding and Neutralising: - To yield is to extend and therefore weaken an incoming force, without losing contact. To neutralise is to nullify that force. To understand yielding and neutralising, we have to consider two verses in the *Wang T'sung-Yueh* classic: "A feather cannot be added", and "A fly cannot settle". These clearly show that even the weight (force) of a feather or fly is enough to set the body in motion. The body should be so sensitive, that it does not allow any force to build on it. The body doesn't pull away from the force, it is the force that sets the body into motion. As a force makes contact with any part of the body, the whole body must change relative to that force, with every part of the body synchronised.

Learning to yield and neutralise is firstly being able to sense the force when it is on your body. You observe your reaction to it, and yield by moving back in the same direction as the force, thereby extending your partner, then neutralise by either turning around your central axis to change the direction of the force or by taking it into the ground. This clears your body of any force, and disconnects the person pushing from his or her own root.

As you progress, you develop the ability to sense when the force is being initiated, usually by your opponents' feet. At this moment your processes of yielding and neutralising synchronise with your opponents' movements, so that by the time they finish releasing their force, you have already nullified it and disconnected them from their root. You are then in a position to *fājìn* (release your own relaxed force).

When you have developed the ultimate *dǒngjìn* (understanding energy), you are able to yield without yielding and neutralise without neutralising, having learnt to understand the force as it approaches. Before your opponent 'releases' physically, they have an intention to move and become mentally committed to it, causing their centre to begin to change. This is an opportunity to disconnect their root, disturb their balance and by simultaneously sending your own force, send them flying.

3.   *Shénmíng* (spiritual clarity):

Often referred to as attaining a state of *tàijí* enlightenment, *shénmíng* represents the pinnacle of the Heaven level.

At this stage the *tīngjìn* (listening) has refined into a kind of intuitive sixth sense, *jiējìn* (receiving energy) has been cultivated, and the *fājìn* (relaxed force) has become almost entirely internal. Like the ultimate in *dǒngjìn*, when your opponents do not move but intend to, you have already moved ahead.

Finally comes the ability to "issue without issuing", which is *fājìn* (releasing the relaxed force) by a subconscious direction of the mind, and without effort.

"A genuine tàijí practitioner can be determined by his tuīshǒu (pushing hands). When a genuine practitioner controls his opponent, the touch is light and yet the opponent is unable to manoeuvre.

When a genuine practitioner discharges, it is without using brute strength, and yet the opponent is catapulted fast and clean, metres away. The person being pushed, might feel the movement but no discomfort.

The genuine practitioner does not grab or hold the opponent, but sticks like glue. The opponent can not get away and feels nothing in the arms. This is real tàijíquán.

Of course it is also possible to control someone or push them away using brute strength, but it is tiring and can leave you breathless. Being pushed by brute strength will feel uncomfortable, and the push will be rough.

On the other hand if someone uses brute strength to push a genuine tàijí practitioner, it will just be like trying to net the wind or catch a shadow. Always coming up empty, like pushing a gourd that is floating on water, the force has nothing to utilise. This is real tàijíquán, so refined that others can only admire."

— ***Yang Cheng-Fu*** *(ref: Chen Wei-Ming Tàijíquán)*

All three of the Heaven level qualities; *tīngjìn*; *dǒngjìn*; and *shénmíng* (described in the previous chapter), are developed through practising a series of two person exercises known as *tuīshǒu* (pushing-hands).

Unfortunately during *tuīshǒu*, many *tàijí* practitioners first think of trying to push their opponents around. This is the main obstacle to developing sensitivity and progressing in *tàijí*, and is therefore a serious mistake. Pushing someone, is not the purpose of *tuīshǒu*, it is only a by-product. The focus must be on the process, not the result.

The objectives of *tuīshǒu* (pushing-hands) practise are:

i.   To train the ability to remain centred, balanced, relaxed, with all your body movements connected and synchronised, while an external force is affecting you.

ii.   To cultivate a sensitivity to forces and an understanding of your reaction to those forces.

iii. To teach you to recognise whether a situation belongs to you or to your partner/opponent.

Tuīshǒu (pushing-hands) training can be divided into four methods:

1.   Fixed *tuīshǒu* (pushing-hands):

The first method of two-person partner work is a series of set patterns. It involves one person playing the role of attacker, and the other as defender, with the roles alternating as the movement circulates. In fixed pushing-hands the direction and timing of the advance to attack and the retreat to neutralise are controlled. Both practitioners learn the principles of sticking, adhering, non-resisting, non-disconnecting, yielding, neutralising and attacking, which are essential to developing *tīngjìn* (listening force).

The first requirement of fixed pushing-hands is to move and synchronise the body the same way as in the form, including being relaxed, connected, balanced and centred. If any one of these is missing it creates an opportunity to be pushed off, no matter how sensitive you have become.

After learning the sequence of fixed pushing-hands, be careful not to lapse into just performing a mechanical movement, absent of *tīngjìn*. A lifetime of such practise will be pointless. To avoid slipping into mechanical movements, the person who is advancing (attacking) should occasionally stop their movement, at any point. Knowing that they might do this, the retreating (defending) person will have to pay close attention and listen to the movement.

Both partners must create a suitable environment for each other to work on the principles. This establishes good *tuīshǒu* (pushing-hands) habits. My teacher would remind us that if the partner does not provide an environment for you to work on the principles, it is best not to practise with them, otherwise you will develop bad habits.

Demonstration of:
Fixed tuīshǒu (pushing-hands) -
Back of the hand

Demonstration of:
Fixed tuīshǒu (pushing-hands) -
Single shoulder push
also known as no arm push

"What you can feel or see, you do not have to be afraid of, because you can adjust to it. It is what you can't feel or see, that you have to be wary of, because you can't tell what is going to happen."

— ***Huang Sheng-Shyan***

"When the sea is rough and the waves are big, you know that it is dangerous. But when it is calm you must be more careful, as the danger beneath isn't obvious"

— ***Wee Kee-Jin***

2.   **Moving step fixed *tuīshǒu*** (pushing-hands):

Practising this method also involves set-patterned two person forms, however this time it includes foot-work, stepping and changing directions. The timing and direction of attacking and defending are still set within the fixed pattern, and the roles interchange.

The principles of sticking, adhering, non-resisting, non-disconnecting, neutralising, yielding and attacking must again be observed to further cultivate *tīngjìn*.

In the Huang system we have two set patterns; the *xiǎolù* (developed by *Huang Sheng-Shyan*); and the *dàlù* for this practice.

This page - demonstration of:

Moving step tuīshǒu (pushing-hands) -
first two steps of xiǎolù (small path)

Far page - demonstration of:

Moving step tuīshǒu (pushing-hands) -
first three steps of dàlù (big path)

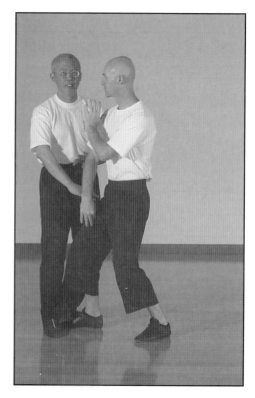

"Being able to uproot someone so that both feet leave the ground, is only the beginning of understanding tuīshǒu (pushing-hands)."

— *Huang Sheng-Shyan*

"Big and unnecessary movements create gaps and chances for your opponent. Tàijí is an efficient martial art, always using the shortest distance, minimum movement, taking the briefest time, and using the least effort to achieve the optimum outcome."

— *Wee Kee-Jin*

3. Semi free *tuīshǒu* (pushing-hands):

This method is a progression from the fixed *tuīshǒu* (pushing-hands) into the free *tuīshǒu* (pushing-hands). In this practice the direction and timing of attacking or defending is not fixed.

However, only one person is attacking at a time, the other only yielding and neutralising. Usually the roles alternate after three to five plays.

The person defending is not going to push, so his or her total focus can be on *tīngjìn*, including listening to your own reaction to the incoming force and how to yield and neutralise that force.

Learning to receive the force is the foundation of yielding and neutralising. When receiving the force, you are working on taking the force into the ground (sinking) and developing a root (grounding). You can remain centred, balanced and relaxed, only when you can totally empty the force from your body into the ground.

The person who is neutralising, learns to react to forces from different directions and at different speeds, as neither is set. The sticking, adhering, not resisting, and not disconnecting are therefore experienced in different situations.

To physically yield and neutralise but be mentally planning an attack, is already resisting.

Not having to worry about being pushed themselves, provides the attacker with time to listen to their partner's and their own, substantiality and insubstantiality. Pushing in this practise is a privilege, and must not involve attacks just for the sake of it. It is more important to learn sticking, adhering, and not disconnecting. When you feel the partner's substantiality, you must not rush in or shove. Rather you should first break the root and then *fājìn* (release the force) in the same relaxed manner that you train the *tàijí* form.

The push must originate in the feet, and pass through the legs into the body, arms and fingers in one connected and unified movement. If pushing to the side, the turning of the hips and waist must provide the direction, not the twisting of the body. Throughout the movement you must remain centred and connected, including after the push. The contact points for releasing the force should not be restricted to the hands, any part of the body can be utilised when "folding".

"A good tàijí push is when your opponent does not feel your push, both his feet are uprooted from the ground, and when he lands on the floor he is still smiling."

— *Huang Sheng-Shyan*

4.   Free *tuīshǒu* (pushing-hands):

In free *tuīshǒu* (pushing-hands), the direction and timing of attacking and defending are not fixed, and both parties can do either at any time. This is the most challenging stage in *tàijí* training, where a vast majority of *tàijí* practitioners forgo the *tàijí* principles and resort to locking, grabbing, resisting, digging in, choking or wrestling. The reason that many adopt these non-*tàijí* practices is having egos with the attitude of winning at all cost.

To progress in free *tuīshǒu* (pushing-hands) it is necessary to overcome your pride. Just as the *Wang Ts'ung – Yueh* classic advises, "…forget oneself, and follow the other". Follow the conscious mind and let it be natural.

Some teachers discourage free *tuīshǒu* (pushing-hands) due to the tendency of students to play rough, or being concerned that they might form bad habits. Yet you wouldn't prevent a language student from writing an essay, just because they might make spelling or grammatical mistakes. Although in fixed *tuīshǒu* (pushing-hands) it is better to train with partners in very controlled environment, in free-pushing it is equally important to learn to deal with a variety of approaches.

The right way to treat free pushing training is to first recognise your own bad practises and correct them before they develop into habits. It is better to be pushed off while following the *tàijí* principles, than to push someone else off without using *tàijí* principles.

You should analyse your practice after each *tuīshǒu* (pushing-hands) training session, learning to recognise what you did, that you shouldn't have, and what you didn't do, which you should have. This analysis will help to develop good habits and eliminate bad ones.

To attain the highest level in *tuīshǒu* (pushing-hands), you must have one hundred percent faith in the *tàijí* principle of relaxation and not use brute strength. Even having ninety-nine point nine percent is not enough, as the point one percent of doubt will cause tension or resistance.

In *tuīshǒu* (pushing-hands), the timing, direction, velocity and resulting distance of the push is not determined by the person pushing, but by the opponent.

The reason that there is not may *tàijí* practitioners who reach a high and refined level in *tuīshǒu* (pushing-hands), is because once they can uproot someone in their push (both feet off the ground), they believe they have mastered it. *Huang Sheng-Shyan* considered this as only the beginning of understanding *tuīshǒu* (pushing-hands).

Demonstration of:

Free tuīshǒu
(pushing-hands)

Jiējìn (receiving energy)

According to *Huang Sheng-Shyan*, the difference between *tàijí* and other martial arts, is that *tàijí* can ultimately develop *jiējìn* (receiving energy), where yielding, neutralising and discharging, all happen simultaneously. There is hardly any physical movement, and no mental intention at all, everything happens spontaneously and naturally.

The practitioner is in a state of absolute central equilibrium, the posture is totally connected and relaxed with the feet deeply rooted. The mind is calm and as still as a mountain. By being totally centred, connected and relaxed the body has become an empty void. When an external force contacts, the body does not resist it, the force just passes through until it hits the ground and rebounds back throwing the opponent. Similar to pile driving during construction work, the deeper the pile is driven into the earth, the higher the hammer rebounds.

Achieving *jiējìn* (receiving energy) indicates attaining *shénmíng* (*tàijí* enlightenment), at which point *sànshǒu* (sparring) techniques become irrelevant.

Demonstration of:
Jiējìn using péng
(ward-off)

The *jìn* (relaxed force) of *tàijí* is not cultivated in the *tuīshǒu* (pushing-hands), it is cultivated in the *tàijí* form. Practising the *tàijí* form is just like running a generator to produce power, whereas pushing-hands is like the appliances utilising that electricity. The appliances are of little use, without the existence of electricity to power them.

The *jìn* (relaxed force) will only develop if the movements in the form are practised with accurate structural alignment, and are connected, synchronised, relaxed plus include sinking.

In the *fājìn* practice, the focus should be on your own connection, rather than on trying to push your partner. Particularly focus on connecting the feet to the ground, body to the base and arms to the body. Then you will be able to connect into your partner's root. Maintain this throughout the transition into posture, once in position, and both during and after the actual release.

In all three of the following two person exercises, one partner (**B**) provides an environment (acts as the *tàijí* sandbag) for the other partner (**A**) to practise the *fājìn*. **B** adopts the bow (archer) stance feet shoulder width apart. Both arms are folded across the body, one palm over the elbow, and the other under it. **B** must not lean against **A**, even when incoming force is detected, otherwise **A** will be pushing against the body weight. If the person (**A**) that is doing the *fājìn* feels that his partner is leaning on him (or her), there is no need to push, all that is necessary is to withdraw and **B** will fall off balance. **B** must also not sit back from the force, otherwise the distance could extend beyond **A**'s reach, to the point where **A** cannot practise the release. **B** must remain in a bow stance, when **B** feels the force coming in, **B** has to relax the body and visualise the force travelling through the body into the ground, under both feet. **B** is therefore practising receiving the force by working on the sinking and grounding (rooting).

1.   **Stationery *fājìn*** (Slow Push):

The purest *Fājìn* is a release of stored force, without propelling yourself forward beyond your centre, or thrusting out the arms.

The slow *fājìn* exercise should be practised on both sides, and if no partner is available, it can be trained by pushing against a wall.

A adopts the bow (archer's) stance, with the front foot parallel to the front foot of **B**, and the front big toe pointing towards **B**'s back heel. **A**'s back foot is forty-five degrees inward with the back heel in line with the big toes of **B**'s front foot.

A places both palms on *B*'s forearms, the little finger just inside *B*'s elbows.

A then sits back along the centre line, keeping upright with the palms remaining in contact with *B*, until ninety percent of the weight is on the back foot.

A moves forward by relaxing both feet, ankles, dropping the knees and seating both hips vertically, to create a downward and forward movement. *A* should experience compression building up in the back leg. It is important to keep the tail bone tucked under, with the body upright and a consciousness on the crown of the head, as if suspended from above. The shoulders must relax and elbows drop to ensure that there is no build up of tension in the body, arms and fingers.

The forward movement finishes when the front knee vertically aligns with the front toes and the weight distribution is fifty-five percent on the back foot. This is the point of optimum compression, just prior to releasing.

A discharges the stored energy by a small downward press of the back foot into the ground and an additional tucking under of the tail bone. During this time both *kuà* (hip joints) must stay seated, and the body relaxed. The back leg only straightens fractionally, with the rear knee staying in line with the back foot and not collapsing inwards. Care needs to be taken to ensure that the front knee remains above the toes and is not propelled further forwards. It is also important not to decrease the connection of either foot with the ground, over the whole sole. The arms only extend from the relaxing and sinking of the shoulders, and the closing (dropping) of the elbows.

Providing that the front *kuà* (hip joint) stays relaxed and seated, the compression released from the back foot can simultaneously sink into the front foot. Subsequently another wave of force can be released from the front foot, again by sinking. In accordance with the principle of cross-alignment, the force from the left foot is released through the right arm, and the force from the right foot is released through the left arm. However the forces from both feet are released in such close succession, that it appears to be together, and both palms remain balanced.

Demonstration of:
Slow fājìn (push) -
connecting into
the partners base

Demonstration of:
Slow fājìn (push) -
breaking the root while
moving forwards

Demonstration of:
Slow fājìn (push) -
releasing the
relaxed force

The mental process within the Stationery Push:

When moving into the bow stance prior to releasing the force, **A** should send a wave of awareness flowing from the crown of the head down through the body, through the legs and into the ground under both feet. When releasing the force, **A** should visualise the mind awareness rebounding from the ground under both feet, up through the *yǒngquán* (bubbling well), into the legs, through the body, shoulders, arms into the palms and fingers. During and after the release, **A** needs to continue projecting the mind from the point of contact, passing through and behind **B**, as far as possible.

2.   **Step in *fājìn*:**

A begins in an upright position with both heels together and the feet pointing forty-five degrees outward.

If *A* is to push with the left foot at the rear, *A* first steps out diagonally with the left foot. Then while dropping into the left leg (knee bending to build up compression), *A* steps directly forward with the right foot so that the heel is in a straight line from where the toes had been.

Simultaneous to the stepping of the right foot, *A* raises both arms. The moment the right foot touches the ground, and the right knee aligns with the front toes, the palms touch *B*'s forearms (the same contact points as described in the stationery push). When the front foot arrives, *A* immediately releases the compression from the back leg.

As in all *fājìn*, the body must remain upright and relaxed with the tail bone tucked in, shoulders relaxed and sunk, elbows dropped, and both *kuà* (hip joints) seated throughout. During the release of the force, extra care must be taken to ensure that the front hip remains relaxed and seated, so that the force from the front foot can also be released.

The weight distribution begins at fifty-five percent on the back foot and forty-five on the front and the front knee remains in line with the front toes. The body should not be propelled further forwards and there should not be any decrease in grounding, both during and after the release of the force.

To help *B* practise receiving the force into the ground instead of resisting it, when *A* is in the position, instead of releasing, *A* should occasionally withdraw both hands. If *B* is leaning against the push or anticipating it, *B* will fall forwards.

To ensure that *A* isn't using upper body strength to push with, sometimes as *A* is about to release, *B* should step away. *A* should remain centred and grounded, and not loose his or her balance.

In *fājìn* practice, if the force is from the feet and connected through the legs, body and arms then both the feet of your partners should be picked off the ground. If your partner just staggers backwards, then it is either not connected, or just a shove using upper body strength.

The mental process of step in *fājìn*:

While stepping with the right foot (having first stepped out with the left foot), *A* sends a wave of mind awareness flowing downward from the crown of the head, through the body into the left leg and into the ground, under the left foot. The moment the right foot touches the ground *A* sends a second wave of mind awareness from the crown of the head through the body into both legs and into the ground under both feet. During the release, *A* should visualise the mind awareness rebounding from the ground under both feet, up through the *yǒngquán* (bubbling well), into the legs, through the body, shoulders, down arms, through the palms and fingers, into *B* and then be projected beyond the partner. When *B* feels the force coming, he or she should visualise taking the force down through the body into the ground, under both feet.

Demonstration of:
Step-in fājìn (push)

Demonstration of:
*Step-in fājìn (push) -
stepping out left foot*

Demonstration of:
*Step-in fājìn (push) -
stepping right foot*

Demonstration of:
*Step-in fājìn (push) -
front foot and hands
arriving simultaneously
breaking the root*

Demonstration of:
*Step-in fājìn (push) -
releasing while
remaining upright*

Demonstration of:
*Step-in fājìn (push) -
continuing to project
the mind*

3. *Fājìn* from the front foot

B adopts the same bow stances as the previous *fājìn* exercises with the left foot at the rear.

A steps out diagonally with his left foot, as the left foot touches the ground, the left leg bends and all of the body weight is dropped into it, creating a compression (and storing of energy). *A* then immediately steps the right foot directly forward.

This is the same as the step in the previous exercise, including simultaneously raising the arms. However this time, the moment the right foot touches the ground, *A* continues relaxing into both *kuà* (hips), and sinking the whole body weight into the front foot, so that the back (left) foot can be drawn in, half-way (diagonally towards the front foot).

The hands make contact with *B*'s forearms and force is released while the left foot is being drawn in. The release is transferred through the body into the arms, palms and fingers, by relaxing and sinking the shoulders and dropping the elbows.

The front *kuà* (hip) must stay seated when the back foot is being drawn in, and the body remains upright. There should not be any decrease in the grounding of the front foot after the release.

Mental process of *fājìn* from the front foot:

When stepping out the right foot, *A* should send a wave of mind awareness from the crown of the head through the body into the ground under the left foot.

When the right foot touches the ground and during the left foot being drawn in, *A* sends a second wave of mind awareness from the crown of the head through the body, down the right leg and into the ground under the right foot. As *B* is pushed off *A* should continue to maintain focus, projecting beyond *B*.

As the force comes in, *B* should visualise taking the force from the contact point, through the body, into the ground under both feet.

Demonstration of:
Fājìn from front foot -
stepping in as before

Demonstration of:
*Fājìn from front foot -
front foot and hands
arriving simultaneously
breaking the root*

Demonstration of:
*Fājìn from front foot -
releasing while bringing
in the back foot*

Demonstration of:
*Fājìn from front foot -
continuing to project
the mind*

Standing exercises are only beneficial after having learned to be relaxed and loose, and once it is understood what to look for. If it is practised before then, the posture will usually only be "held up" using body tension, and a habit of internal resistance consequently develops. This is the absolute opposite, to the purpose of the practice.

The primary aim of the standing exercise, is to cultivate a root through grounding. In addition it serves the purpose of developing awareness of the physical and mental connections within the structure, the centre of equilibrium, and the process of releasing tension.

There are three postures in the *tàijí* form that we generally use for the standing exercise. They are the preparation posture, single whip and the raise arms.

### 1.	**The Preparation** Posture:

The importance of the preparation position as a standing exercise, is emphasised by *Cheng Man-ch'ing* in his book "The Thirteen Chapters". In it he says that, "Most practitioners neglect this posture, little do they know that the way and application of *tàijí* is in this posture".

Stand with the feet a shoulder width apart, the outside of the soles parallel to each other and vertically aligned to the shoulders. The legs are bent so that both knees are in line with the front toes. The body is upright and the *wěilǘ* (tail bone) is tucked in. There needs to be a light consciousness of the crown of the head, visualising it to be suspended from above. Both *kuà* (hip joints) are relaxed and seated, chest softened from within. Arms are by the sides of the body, with the wrists seated and palms facing down. Both thumbs and index fingers are in contact with the thighs and all fingers slant forwards. The awareness of the hands is at the *láogōng* meridian points in the centre of the palms. The shoulders need to be relaxed and sunk, the elbows dropped but not collapsed. The arms form an arc with the sides of the body. The mouth is naturally closed, with the tip of tongue lightly in contact with the roof of the mouth, just behind the teeth.

The Mental Process of the Standing Exercise:

Once the physical structure is established, bring the mental focus within, freeing the mind of other thoughts. Then, cultivate the awareness of the physical connection of the structure by sending the mind awareness into the feet. Ensure that the toes are relaxed, not gripping against the floor, both *yǒngquán* (bubbling well) are in contact with the ground, with body weight evenly

Demonstration of:

*Standing exercise - preparation posture
with hands in closed position*

Demonstration of:

*Standing exercise - preparation posture
wrists seated at the thigh*

distributed over both feet. There should be a feeling of strong connection of the feet with the floor. Visualise grounding into the floor, sending the mental sinking into the earth under the both feet. The feet are the root and must remain connected at all times to be able to "borrow the energy from the earth".

Next bring the mind awareness into the thighs, using visualisation to cultivate the release of tension from the muscles (quadriceps). If there is any tension in the thighs, it will reduce the amount of relaxation possible in the upper body. Move the awareness to the *kuà* (hips joint) checking that they are seated so that the upper body can connect with the base. Use the mind awareness to cultivate the relaxation of the upper body muscles, softening the chest from within. Become aware of the shoulders, ensuring that they are relaxed and sunk so that the arms can connect with the body. Then visualise the arms, palms and fingers, to be free of all tension.

Next align to the centre of equilibrium. Using your mind awareness, verify that the *wěilú* (tail bone) is tucked in, the body is upright, and the chin is drawn in, while remaining lightly consciousness of the *níwán* (crown of the head) as if suspended from above. Visualise a line extending from the crown of the head through the body, connecting to the *huìyīn* (a meridian point between the anus and groin), and project the line downward to a point between two feet. This serves as the central axis of the body, by visualising it vertical, and aligning the body to it, it becomes the centre of equilibrium.

Lastly, sink a wave of mind awareness flowing down from the *níwán* (crown of the head), through the body (including the arms), the legs, the feet and into the *yǒngquán* (bubbling well) and deep into the ground under both feet. As that mind awareness passes through the body, visualise the different parts to melt, which will produce an increase in the grounding of the feet, particularly when the awareness passes into the ground.

Keep repeating the cycles of checking the physical connection, aligning to the centre of equilibrium and mentally sinking, throughout the entire duration of the standing exercise.

The qualities of the physically connecting, aligning to the centre of equilibrium and the mentally sinking, that are cultivated in this standing exercise, must eventually be also present in the *tàijí* form movements, throughout the transitions, when in position, and during the release of relaxed force.

2.   **Single Whip** Standing Posture:

The purpose of single whip standing posture is to work on the opening and expanding of the joints and the lateral (from the side) stability of the structure.

Adopt a bow (archer) stance; feet shoulder width apart, the back foot (toes) turned inwards forty-five degrees, with the back knee in line with the big toe of the back foot (this is to keep the back hip joint open and the sole of the back foot in full contact with the ground). Weight distributed fifty-five percent on the back foot, forty-five on the front. The front foot should be straight on the outside of the sole and the front knee aligns with the front toes. Both *kuà* (hips) should be relaxed

and seated, the body upright and relaxed, chest softened from within, both shoulders relaxed and sunk. The elbow of the front (left) arm should be dropped, hand placed within the width of the shoulders with the palm facing diagonally downward. The thumb tip is in line with the central axis of the body, and the arc between the thumb and index finger is at shoulder height. The (right) arm should be extended outward with the wrist at shoulder height. The hand is hooked position with all four fingers enclosing the thumb. The elbow is dropped to a depth of two finger widths below the shoulder (and wrist) level. The body and the hips are square to the direction faced.

Once the physical structure is established begin the mental process, following the same steps as for the previous standing posture by repeating the cycles of checking the physical connection, aligning to the centre of equilibrium, and mentally sinking.

3.   **Raise Arms** Standing Posture:

This standing posture is to develop the central equilibrium while lifting and closing.

The back (left) foot is turned inwards fifteen degrees and supports the whole body weight, toes relaxed, weight evenly distributed over the whole sole, the *yǒngquán* (bubbling well) connected to the floor. The heel of the other (right) foot is directly in front of the left heel and although in contact with the ground, bears no body weight; the toes are off the floor. The back leg is bent at the knee, whereas the front leg is straight but the knee is unlocked. The body should be upright and relaxed with the tail bone tucked in, conscious of the crown of the head (as if the head is being

Far page -
demonstration of:
Single Whip - standing posture
to both directions

This page & following page -
demonstration of:
Raise Arms - standing posture
alternating legs and arms

suspended from the top). The *kuà* (hips) should be seated and both shoulders relaxed and sunk.

When the left foot is the back foot, then the right arm is extended with the elbow dropped and the arc of the thumb and index finger at shoulder height, in line with the central axis of the body and the palm facing slightly upward.

The left thumb is about one fist width from the right elbow, with the palm facing slightly upward. The left elbow is dropped, one fist distance away from the trunk of the body.

Once the physical structure is established begin the mental process. The cycles are similar to those in the other two standing postures, except that in the physical connection; only the back foot is firmly connected to the ground, and in the mental sinking; the mind awareness is only projected under the back foot.

Regardless of the different styles, all *tàijíquán* is based on the following *tàijí* classics[1]:

i)   Chang San-Feng *Tàijí* Classic
ii)   Wang Ts'ung–Yueh *Tàijí* Classic
iii) The Song of Thirteen Postures
iv)   Understanding of the Thirteen Postures
v)   The Song of *Tuīshǒu* (Pushing-hands)
vi)   Important *Tàijí* points from the *Yang* family
vii) The Song of Substance and Function.

All *tàijí* styles originate from the same source, perhaps taking a different path but meeting at the same destination. All practitioners should constantly refer to the classics to ensure that they don't disconnect from the source. If one person performs the whole *tàijí* form while not following the principles contained in the classics, and someone else only repeats a single movement yet adheres to the classical principles, the second practitioner is the only one truly performing *tàijí*.

Progress in *tàijí* is a reflection of the amount of time put into training, together with an understanding of the classics and the ability to put them into practice. Therefore by developing a deeper understanding of the *tàijí* principles, your *tàijí* naturally progresses.

An instructor is only a medium for the *tàijí* wisdom to be transmitted through, the real teacher is the classics. It is important that the instructor avoids deviating from the principles within the *tàijí* classics, just as it is the responsibility of the students to follow what the classics state, and not necessarily the teacher's interpretation. Therefore both teacher and student should constantly be referring to the classic texts.

---

[1]Reference (not the origin of the classics, but the Chinese version most closely referred to):

Title:	*Zhèngzǐ tàijíquán shísān piān*	*Cheng's* Thirteen Chapters on *Tàijíquán*
Author:	*Zhèng Mànqīng*	*Cheng Man-ch'ing*
Publisher:	*Lánxī tú shū chū bǎn yǒu xiàn gōng sī*	*Lánxī* Publishing Company Ltd - *Taiwan*
Published:	*Yī jiǔ jiǔ èr nián liù yuè (bā shuā)*	June 1992 (8th reprint)

太 極 拳 論

1. 一舉動，周身俱要輕靈，尤須貫串。

2. 氣宜鼓盪，神宜內斂。

3. 無使有缺陷處。
   無使有凹凸處。
   無使有斷續處。

4. 其根在腳，發於腿。
   主宰於腰，形於手指。
   由腳而腿而腰，總須完整一氣。

5. 向前退後，乃能得機得勢。
   有不得機得勢處，身便散亂。
   其病必於腰腿求之。

6. 上下前後左右皆然。
   凡此皆是意，不在外面。

7. 有上即有下，有前則有後，有左則有右。
   如意要向上，即寓下意。

8. 若將物掀起，而加以挫之之力。
   斯其根自斷，乃壞之速而無疑。

9. 虛實宜分清楚。
   一處有一處虛實，處處總此一虛實。

10. 周身節節貫串，無令絲毫間斷耳。

11. 長拳者，如長江大海，滔滔不絕也。

1.   Throughout all movements, the body should be light, agile and most importantly connected together [synchronised].

2.   The *qì* should be stimulated and the *shén* (spirit) gathered within.

3.   Do not have deficient places. Do not have any hollow or protruding places. Do not have disconnected places.

4.   The root [of the relaxed force] is in the feet, discharged through the legs, controlled by the waist, and expressed through to the fingers. From the feet through the legs to the waist, should be one flow of *qì*.

5.   Therefore when moving forwards and backwards you will have flexibility and momentum. If there is no flexibility or momentum, and the body becomes disrupted, the fault should be sought in the waist and legs.

6.   Up or down, forwards and backwards, left or right, are all the same. All these are within the mind and not physically manifested.

7.   If there is up, there must be down. If there is forwards there must be backwards. If there is left, there must be right. If the mind has an upward intention, simultaneously it must have a downward intention.

8.   In lifting the opponent, first connect down, by doing so breaking the root, so that he can be plucked out in a flash of a moment.

9.   Substantial and insubstantial should be clearly differentiated. In every part there is both substantial and insubstantial. The principle of substantial and insubstantial applies to every situation.

10.   The whole body should be connected together, joint by joint like string. Do not allow the slightest disruption.

11.   The *chángquán* (long fist: an earlier description of *tàijíquán*) practitioner is like a river or ocean, continuously flowing and rolling without end.

12. 掤攦擠按採挒肘靠，此八卦也。

13. 進步退步左顧右盼中定，此五行也。

14. 掤攦擠按，即乾坤坎離，四正方也。

15. 採挒肘靠，即巽震兌艮，四斜角也。

16. 進退顧盼定，即金木水火土也。合之則為十三勢也。

17. 原註云。此係武當山張三丰祖師遺論。
    欲天下豪傑延年益壽。不徒作技藝之末也。

12. *Péng* (ward-off), *lǔ* (roll-back), *jǐ* (press), and *àn* (push), *cǎi* (pluck), *liè* (split), *zhǒu* (elbow-strike) and *kào* (lean-on) represent the eight trigrams.

13. Step forward, sit backward, look left, look right, centralised, relate to the five elements.

14. *Péng* (ward-off), *lǔ* (roll-back), *jǐ* (press), and *àn* (push) relate to *qián, kūn, kǎn* and *lí*. These represent the four cardinal directions.

15. *Cǎi* (pluck), *liè* (split), *zhǒu* (elbow-strike) and *kào* (lean-on) relate to *xùn, zhèn, duì* and *gěn*, being the four diagonals.

16. Step forward, sit backward, look left, look right and centralised are represented by metal, wood, water, fire, and earth respectively. All together these make up the thirteen postures.

17. The original annotation: This classic was left by the [legendary] founder, *Chang San-Feng* of *Wudang* mountain. The intended purpose was for the followers to attain health and longevity, not just for combat.

1. The moment you move, the body should be agile. In order to have agility, the body must maintain its centre of equilibrium while in position, as well as during transitions. To synchronise requires an understanding of the sequence of changes that create the movements. Then time the sequences to change in relation to one another, as connected movements, not just co-ordinated actions.

2. Use mind awareness to stimulate the *qì* and circulate it throughout the body. The mind motivates the *qì*. The *shén* (spirit - focus) should be brought within the body, to prevent the attention from wandering off.

3. Deficiencies in *tàijí* include not maintaining the *zhōng zhèng* (centre of equilibrium), not being *sōng* (relaxed), not turning from the *kuà* (hips) and *yāo* (waist) and being *duàn* (disconnected). In *tuīshǒu* (pushing-hands) using *lì* (brute strength), resisting, not sticking or adhering are also deficiencies. To avoid deficiencies, every word in the *tàijí* classics should be strictly followed.

    The movement should be smooth and circular. Hunching the back (concaving the upper spine) or protruding the buttocks (a convex curve in the lower spine), results in the body being out of alignment and disconnected from the base. Any discontinuity in the movement prevents parts of the body synchronising, and provides opportunities for *tuīshǒu* (pushing-hands) opponents .

4. The *yǒngquán* (bubbling well) in the feet is the root of the body structure. When the feet are firmly grounded (rooted) you connect to "borrow the energy of the earth", and any incoming force can be neutralised by being emptied into the ground. The upper body will be free to relax, agile and able to maintain the *zhōngzhèng* (central equilibrium) with ease.

    The 'Song of Substance and Function' states that, "if the *yǒngquán* (bubbling well) has no root, the *yāo* (waist) has no control". To cultivate the root in the feet, it is essential to relax the toes, not grip the floor, distribute the weight evenly over the whole sole, and soften the arch until the *yǒngquán* (bubbling well) is in contact with the ground.

    Whenever practising *chén* (sinking) in the *tàijí* form, the mind awareness must be sent into the feet through the *yǒngquán* (bubbling well), and projected deep into the ground.

    Once the feet are firmly rooted, bring the *jìn* (relaxed force) through the legs. The *yāo* (waist), positioned by turning from the hips, determines the direction of the discharge. The *jìn* (relaxed force) is then transferred into the upper body by drawing under the tail-bone and keeping the hips seated, down the arms by dropping the shoulders, and 'melting' the upper body, through the palms and into the finger-tips.

From the feet to the legs and onto the waist is a continuous synchronised movement and wave of mind awareness, therefore one flow of *qì* without break.

5. If moving forwards and backwards is hindered or unsynchronised, there will be a disconnection preventing the body from moving as one. The cause is likely to be the position of the legs in relation to the upper body or the *yāo* (waist) having lost its mobility from the *kuà* (hips) being locked or not seated into the pelvic sockets.

6. Sometimes in *tàijí*, up and down, forwards and backwards, left and right are not physical movements, but only mind intentions.

7. Everything is relative to its opposite. If there is *yīn*, there is *yáng*; if there is up, there must also be down; if there is forwards, there must also be backwards; and if there is left, there must also be right.

    In *tuīshǒu* (pushing-hands) when you draw people up to a point where they begin to lose connection, they will most likely withdraw downwards. When you draw people forwards beyond their centre, they will attempt to sit back. When you lead people to the left further than their balance allows, they are likely to turn back to the right. In all of the previous situations the moment of change of direction is an opportunity to take advantage of, when the opponent can be easily toppled.

    To maintain grounding and a connection to your own and opponents root, as the mind has an upward intention there must simultaneously be another wave of mind awareness sent deep into the earth. Otherwise you will actually be uprooting yourself.

8. To lift an opponent you first must send your mind awareness into the feet of the opponent to break the root. Once the root is broken, pushing in any direction is an easy matter.

9. It is essential to distinguish both your own and your partners' substantiality and insubstantiality. When executing *fājìn* (releasing the relaxed force) from the right substantial foot, the principle of cross-alignment requires that it be transmitted through the left substantial arm and vice-versa. The *jìn* (relaxed force) should be directed into the root of your opponent, which is located beneath his or her substantial foot. When your opponent's substantial force contacts any part of your body, that point must immediately become insubstantial. Substantial and insubstantial are not simply one being left and the other right or similarly up and down, both are present in every part of the body, constantly interchanging, rebalancing and adjusting to the situation.

10. To achieve whole body synchronisation, every part of the body must move and change while connected to, and in relation with, each other. When complete synchronisation is achieved there is no likelihood of disconnection.

11. In ancient times *tàijíquán* was referred to as *chángquán* (long fist). Regardless of name, when a practitioner performs the form or *tuīshǒu* (pushing-hands), their movements should be like the rolling flow of the river, never ending and leaving no gap for an opponent to enter. The circulation of *qì* (vital energy) is comparable to the currents and tides of the ocean, and the *jìn* (relaxed force) generated, relates to the waves and surf.

12. *Péng* (ward-off), *lǔ* (roll-back), *jǐ* (press), *àn* (push), *cǎi* (pluck), *liè* (split), *zhǒu* (elbow-strike) and *kào* (lean-on) are the four cardinal directions and four diagonal directions respectively. Together they make up the eight trigrams.

13. Step forward, sit backward, look left, look right, central equilibrium, equate to the five elements; metal, wood, water, fire and earth

14. *Péng* (ward-off), *lǔ* (roll-back), *jǐ* (press), and *àn* (push) relate to *qián, kūn, kǎn* and *lí*. These represent the four cardinal directions, which are south, north, west and east.

15. *Cǎi* (pluck), *liè* (split), *zhǒu* (elbow-strike) and *kào* (lean-on) relate to *xùn* (wind), *zhèn* (thunder), *duì* (swamp or lake) and *gèn* (mountain), which are the four diagonals; south-west, north-east, south-east and north-west.

16. Together the four cardinal directions, the four diagonals and the five elements, make up the classical thirteen postures.

17. A notation on the original document states that, "this 'Classic' was left by *Chang San-Feng* from *Wudang* mountain", being the legendary founder and birthplace of *tàijí*. The author goes on to identify the purpose of the art as being for students to live long healthy lives, not simply as a method of fighting.

山西王宗嶽

太極拳經

1. 太極者無極而生。
   陰陽之母也。

2. 動之則分靜之則合。

3. 無過不及隨曲就伸。

4. 人剛我柔謂之走，我順人背謂之黏。

5. 動急則急應，動緩則緩隨。

6. 雖變化萬端，而理為一貫。

7. 由着熟而漸悟懂勁。
   由懂勁而階及神明。

8. 然非功力之久，不能豁然貫通焉。

9. 虛靈頂勁氣沉丹田。

10. 不偏不倚忽隱忽現。

11. 左重則左虛，右重則右杳。

12. 仰之則彌高，俯之則彌深。
    進之則愈長，退之則愈促。

1. *Tàijí* is born from *wújí*.
    It is the mother of *yīn* and *yáng*.

2. In movements it [*yīn* and *yáng*] separates
    and in stillness it unifies.

3. It must not be overdone or fall short.
    Respond to the curve with expansion.

4. When the opposition is strong, become supple; this is yielding.
    Follow the person back without disconnection; this is sticking.

5. When the movement is fast, respond quickly.
    When the movement is slow, follow slowly.

6. Although there are many variations,
    there is only one principle.

7. Proficiency evolves into understanding the forces.
    Understanding precedes spiritual clarity.

8. Only through persevered practice will profound understanding be attained.

9. Be conscious on the crown of the head.
    Sink the *qì* to the *dāntián*.

10. Do not tilt or lean.
    Suddenly conceal and suddenly reveal.

11. When the left is substantial, the left becomes insubstantial and when the right is
    substantial, the right becomes insubstantial.

12. When the opponent attacks upwards, I lead him higher.
    When the opponent attacks downwards, I draw him lower.
    When he steps forward, I over extend him.
    When he withdraws I close onto him.

13. 一羽不能加，蠅蟲不能落。
    人不知我，我獨知人。

14. 英雄所向無敵，蓋皆由此而及也。

15. 斯技旁門甚多，雖勢有區別。
    概不外乎壯欺弱，慢讓快耳。

16. 有力打無力，手慢讓手快。
    是皆先天自然之能，非關學力而有為也。

17. 察四兩撥千斤之句，顯非力勝。
    觀耄耋能禦眾之形，快何能為。

18. 立如平準，活似車輪。
    偏沉則隨，雙重則滯。

19. 每見數年純功，不能運化者，
    率自為人制，雙重之病未悟耳。

20. 欲避此病，須知陰陽相濟，方為懂勁。

21. 懂勁後，愈練愈精，默識揣摩，
    漸至從心所欲。

22. 本是舍己從人，多誤舍近求遠。
    所謂差之毫釐，謬以千里。
    學者不可不詳辨焉。是為論。

13. A feather cannot be added.
    A fly cannot settle.

14. The opponent is not aware of me, but I'm fully aware of him.
    He who has achieved all of this, will be invincible.

15. There are a lot of other marital arts, with differences in styles and movements. However their basis is the strong overcoming the weak or the slow giving way to the fast.

16. The strong overcoming the weak and the slow giving way to the fast, is simply an innate skill and not an achievement of martial art study.

17. Considering the verse; "Only four *tael* are required to neutralise a thousand *catty* of force", shows that victory is not due to superior strength.
    Observing an old man defeating a mob raises the question; what is [the value] of speed?

18. Stand like a level scale, be mobile like a wheel.
    Sinking allows you to follow,
    double heaviness causes you to be stagnant (hindered).

19. Someone after years of dedicated practice being unable to adjust or neutralise, and is easily defeated by others, has not understood the fault of double heaviness.

20. To avoid this fault, you must understand the harmony (dynamic association) between *yīn* and *yáng*. This will lead to *dǒngjìn* (understanding the forces/energies).

21. Once *dǒngjìn* is achieved; further practice and analysis develops greater refinements. Gradually you will reach the stage where everything extends from the will of the mind and *xīn* (heart).

22. The foundation is to forget yourself, and follow the other.
    Most mistakenly neglect the near and pursue the far.
    It is said: "To miss by a fraction of a *lǐ* is to miss by a thousand *lǐ*.
    The student must comprehend all of these points fully,
    so I [*Wang Ts'ung – Yueh*] say.

1. *Wújí* is a state of nothingness, no thoughts nor movements. The moment a thought enters the mind, *wújí* ceases to exist. Then it changes into the state of *tàijí*, which comprises of *yīn* and *yáng* aspects. Therefore *tàijí* is the mother of *yīn* and *yáng*.

2. During movement, *yīn* and *yáng* separate but remain in harmony.
   In stillness they merge.

3. Movements in the *tàijí* form and pushing-hands must not be excessive or deficient. This emphasises the importance of accuracy within the movements. Overdoing or under-doing movements results in locking yourself up or becoming vulnerable to an opponent's attack. These faults cause either the disconnection from, or the obstruction of, the relaxed forces.

   In *tuīshǒu* (pushing-hands) to counter the opponent's neutralisation, cut into their curve and expand in a straight line. This response will negate their neutralisation and enable you to successfully complete your release (bisecting a circle always locates its centre).

4. When the opponent has a strong force, be like a sponge, so supple that the force has nothing to utilise; this is yielding. When the opponent attacks; yield, neutralise and connect behind the direction the force. When he or she realises that they have over-extended and decide to retreat, follow without losing contact with his or her base; this is sticking.

5. The speed of the movements in *tuīshǒu* (pushing-hands) is determined by your opponent. To be able to synchronise with the speed whether fast or slow, you must stick, adhere, follow, not disconnect, not resist and be able to listen to, and understand the forces.

6. Although there are many different movements, the guiding principle is consistent (the same throughout).

7. When you become skilful, you can reach the state of *dǒngjìn* (understanding the forces). *Dǒngjìn* is evident when the opponent does not move; you do not move, when the opponent has the slightest movement; you have already moved ahead. *Dǒngjìn* later evolves into the state of spiritual clarity or *tàijí* enlightenment. At this level even when the opponent does not move, you move ahead. In this case, although there is no apparent physical movement, the opponent has already formed a mental intention to move. Recognising this moment is possible once you have developed the deep sensitivity to 'listen' without depending on physical contact.

8. Spiritual clarity (*tàijí* enlightenment) only comes after many years of consistent practice. *Tàijí* is a life long process.

9. Being conscious of the crown of the head means the same as visualising the head to be suspended from above. The aim is to keep the body erect and upright and control the centre of equilibrium, thereby reducing the likelihood of the chest collapsing (shoulders hunching) when relaxing the body. The *qì* sinks into the *dāntián* by using the mind awareness to guide it there, and must not be done forcefully. The *qì* needs to be gathered and stored in the *dāntián* (the sea of *qì*) before it can be directed to other parts of the body. The ability to sink the *qì* into the *dāntián* represents entering the first stage of the 'Earth' level.

10. The body must be upright and level. Any leaning forwards or backwards or tilting to one side will result in the posture losing its centre of equilibrium. In *tuīshǒu* (pushing-hands), when you have the ability to disguise your intention, the opponent will be confused. Therefore you will know your opponents, but they will not be able to know you. By the time your opponents realise your push is coming, their root is already broken.

11. The *tàijí* theory of the cross-alignment states that the force from the left foot is delivered through the right arm, and conversely the force from the right foot is delivered through the left arm. Releasing the force from the left foot with the left arm or the force from the right foot with the right arm, is regarded as a fault of *shuāngzhòng* (equal heaviness).

12. Over-extending opponents disconnect them from their centre and root. When opponents attack upward; lead them higher than was intended, thereby avoiding places for them to utilise. When opponents attack low, draw them lower by creating an emptiness, causing them to lose their balance. When opponents step forward, over-stretch them to bring them out of their centre. Once the opponents realise that they are out of their centre, they will inevitably withdraw. Then you should immediately follow and close in at such a speed that they will not have a chance to regain themselves.

13. After years of practice you can develop such sensitivity that the weight of a feather or fly will set you in motion. In pushing-hands it is not that you move away from the force, it is the force (feather or fly) that sets you moving. When the level of *dǒngjìn* is achieved, you will be able to be constantly aware of your opponents' forces.

14. When you are able to conceal your intention, your opponents will not be aware of you.

    When you achieve all of the above, there will be no match for your *tàijí* skill. However it is no achievement to merely repeat the theory. Rather the principles must be evident in your body, with you having acquired the ability to apply them practically.

15. There are several kinds of other martial arts (even more if you consider the styles within each). What the training for most of these systems has in common is the emphasis on strength and or speed. Essentially they develop techniques involving stronger forces or greater speeds, to overcome their opponents.

16. The concepts of the weak being overcome by the strong, and the slow giving way to the fast, are not special martial art skills. These are base level instincts, and are utilised in nearly every sporting arena.

17. To understand how the weak can overcome the strong, you have to study the principle of four *tael* dealing with a thousand *catty*. This principle is expressed in the 'Song of *Tuīshǒu*'. When you observe an old *tàijí* adept pushing around numerous younger students, you will see the little value of physical speed. Because of his *tīngjìn* (listening) and *dǒngjìn* (understanding) the adept will know the opponents' intentions before they have even commenced their physical movement. Consequently such an adept is always one step ahead. This is *tàijí* speed.

18. You must be upright and balanced like a level scale to achieve central equilibrium. When you have the mobility of a wheel, you can not get stuck and forces will not be able to land on you. In any movement there must be sinking, so any in-bound force will be absorbed from the body through the feet into the ground. There should be no resistance and no obstruction in the body, so that when you relax, you become grounded. You must develop the ability to follow the opponent without hindrance. Double heaviness results from opposing force with force. Consequently the body tenses up and the grounding is undermined, causing obstruction and immobility.

19. If after years of practice you cannot apply the principles in *tuīshǒu* (pushing-hands) and always get pushed around by your opponents, it is because you have not understood the principle of double heaviness, and its cause.

20. To overcome this fault, harmonise the *yīn* and *yáng*, so that when the opponent is ten percent *yáng*, you are ten percent *yīn* and vice-versa. To do this you must first develop *tīngjìn* and *dǒngjìn* the listening and understanding of the forces.

21. Even after achieving *dǒngjìn* (understanding) you must continue to practice, analyse and refine your practise to achieve the level of *tàijí* enlightenment. At this level, the body will naturally follow the will of the mind and heart (conscience).

22. The foremost principle is to not assert yourself but rather harmonise with your opponent (follow the other). Unfortunately most practitioners ignore the process (the near), and instead look for the result (the far). The accuracy of the movement and the process is more important. If you depart the origin out by a millimetre then you could miss the destination by hundreds of kilometres (in the Chinese 'Old System' of measurement a *lí* approximates to 576m)

According to *Wang T'sung Yueh*; all *tàijí* practitioners should understand the principles fully and clearly.

十三勢歌

1. 十三勢來莫輕視。命意源頭在腰際。

2. 變轉虛實須留意。氣遍身軀不少滯。

3. 靜中觸動動猶靜。因敵變化示神奇。

4. 勢勢存心揆用意。得來不覺費功夫。

5. 刻刻留心在腰間。腹內鬆淨氣騰然。

6. 尾閭中正神貫頂。滿身輕利頂頭懸。

7. 仔細留心向推求。屈伸開合聽自由。

8. 入門引路須口授。功夫無息法自修。

9. 若言體用何為準。意氣君來骨肉臣。

10. 想推用意終何在。益壽延年不老春。

11. 歌兮歌兮百四十。字字真切意無遺。

12. 若不向此推求去。枉費功夫貽歎息。

1. Do not take the song of thirteen postures lightly.
   The source of life is in the waist area.

2. Attention must be paid to the changes of substantial and insubstantial.
   Let the *qì* flow freely throughout the body.

3. Calmness precedes the motion and while in motion, calmness remains. Effectiveness is demonstrated by adapting to the opponent's changes.

4. Using awareness throughout every movement,
   progress comes naturally.

5. Be aware of the waist at all times.
   Relax the abdomen and the *qì* will come alive.

6. Tuck under the tailbone and be conscious of [raise the *shén* to] the crown of the head.
   If the head is held as though suspended by the crown,
   the body will be agile.

7. Pay careful attention in your practice of pushing-hands.
   Let the movement of expanding and contracting, opening and closing be natural.

8. To be shown the route to the [*tàijí*] door you need oral transmission.
   Through continuous practice and self analysis comes the [*tàijí*] method.

9. If asked the principle of the understanding and its application, answer; the *yì* (mind intention) and the *qì* are the kings, while the flesh and bones are their subjects.

10. What is the goal of understanding and its application?
    To keep healthy, and have a long life.

11. This song, this song of one hundred and forty words.
    Every word contains the truth and whole meaning.

12. If you do not adhere to the above,
    your effort will be in vain and only a sigh will result.

1.   The principles found in the song of thirteen postures must be taken seriously, practised diligently and not taken lightly. The waist area is where the kidneys are located, and in traditional Chinese medicine it is believed that the prenatal life force inherited from your parents, is stored there. In *tàijí* the *kuà* (hips) and *yāo* (waist) are the source of upper body mobility.

2.   You must always be aware of your own, and your opponents, expressions of substantiality and insubstantiality. According to the theory of cross-alignment; when the right foot is substantial the left arm is substantial and vice-versa. Another example is; when your opponent is substantial, you should be insubstantial. If your right arm and right foot are substantial at the same time, or you're substantial when your opponent is also substantial, then there is *shuāngzhòng* (equal heaviness - often mistranslated as double weighted). This will severely hinder your movements and the flow of *qì*. When you can understand the changes between what is substantial and what is insubstantial, the *qì* will be able to flow freely throughout the body, by the directive of the mind.

3.   The mind should be calm to motivate the *qì*, which in turn motivates the physical movement. During the movement the mind should not drift off, it should be entirely present within the movement. When the mind is calm throughout the *tàijí* form, you can understand the changes that create every movement, and you can be aware of any tension in the body. During *tuīshǒu* (pushing-hands), the calm mind provides you with the opportunity to 'hear' your opponents every move, and understand your reaction to it.

If you're able to adapt to the opponent's changes, the force will have nowhere to land. To be able to adapt to the changes of the opponent, you must be able to understand the principles of, and listen to, the changes between *yīn* (insubstantial) and *yáng* (substantial), while sticking, adhering, not resisting and not disconnecting.

4.   Correct practice will produce natural progress. Correct practice includes having awareness of; - the movements; the sequence that creates the movement; the timing of the changes; the connection; the centre of equilibrium while moving; and the relaxation and sinking within the movement.

5.   The waist controls the direction of the upper body. Therefore any change in the direction of the upper body must originate from the waist. If the abdomen is relaxed then the *qì* will

naturally sink and gather in the *dāntián*. The *qì* can then be directed from the *dāntián* to every part of the body.

6. When the tail bone is tucked under and the consciousness is on the crown of the head, the *níwán (bǎihùi)* and the *huìyīn* are aligned and the central axis within the body is established. While centre of equilibrium is maintained, visualising the head to be suspended from above decreases the likelihood of collapsing the chest or hunching the back. When the centre of equilibrium is achieved the body is centred, balanced, and therefore agile when moving.

7. To cultivate *tīngjìn* (listening) and *dǒngjìn* (understanding) of the forces; pay close attention to the practice of pushing-hands, developing sticking, adhering, and following, while not disconnecting or resisting. When the above is achieved, the body will expand and contract, open and close naturally, without premeditation.

8. Beginners in *tàijí* require a knowledgeable teacher to impart the *tàijí* knowledge to them. Books and videos can only serve as references, and cannot actually teach you *tàijí*. Progress only comes from practice and self analysis. Learning without practising, is like eating without digesting.

9. Question: What is the main principle of the understanding and application? Answer: The subject / body (flesh and bone) must follow the commands of the king - *yì* (mind intention) and *qì*. In every movement the mind, motivates the *qì*, and the *qì* motivates the body.

10. The main aim of understanding and applying the *tàijí* principles is to cultivate a healthy and long life.

11. In the original Chinese text (original) the 'song' has twenty verses each with seven words, making a total of one hundred and forty words. The meaning of every word is clear and important.

12. If you do not follow the principles contained in this 'song' and base your practice on it, your effort will not achieve anything.

十三勢行功心解

1. 以心行氣。務令沉着。乃能收斂入骨。

2. 以氣運身。務令順遂。乃能便利從心。

3. 精神能提得起。則無遲重之虞。所謂頂頭懸也。

4. 意氣須換得靈。乃有圓活之趣。所謂轉變虛實也。

5. 發勁須沉着鬆淨。專主一方。

6. 立身須中正安舒。支撐八面。

7. 行氣如九曲珠。無往不利。
   （氣遍身軀之謂）運勁如百煉鋼，無堅不摧。

8. 形如搏兔之鶻。神如捕鼠之貓。

9. 靜如山岳。動如江河。

10. 蓄勁如張弓。發勁如放箭。

11. 曲中求直。蓄而後發。

12. 力由脊發。步隨身換。

1. The *xīn* (mind/heart) motivates the *qì*, directs it to sink, so that it can be stored and concentrated into the bones.

2. Let the *qì* motivate the body without hindrance, so that it will effortlessly follow your *xīn* (mind/heart).

3. If the *shén* (spirit) is raised, there will not be any sluggishness. This is the meaning of the crown of the head being suspended from above.

4. There should be agility in the interaction of the *yì* (mind intention) and *qì*, so that it [the *qì*] will be circular and lively. This is what is meant by, 'changing substantial and insubstantial'.

5. When executing *fājìn* (releasing the force) the body should relax and sink. Focus on the one direction.

6. When the body is upright, loose and tranquil, the feet will support all eight directions.

7. Direct the *qì* like threading the 'nine bend pearls',
    by flowing continuously it reaches everywhere unrestricted.

    [When the *qì* flows throughout the body] the *jìn* (relaxed force) is like tempered steel, overcoming all solid defences.

8. Have the appearance of a falcon preying on a hare.
    Concentrate the *shén* (spirit) like a cat stalking a mouse.

9. Be calm like a mountain and move like a river.

10. Store up the *jìn* (relaxed force) like drawing a bow,
    discharge the *jìn* (relaxed force) like releasing an arrow.

11. Seek the straight in the curve,
    first store then discharge.

12. Force is released through the back,
    the steps change with the body.

13. 收即是放，斷而復連。

14. 往復須有摺疊。進退須有轉換。

15. 極柔軟。然後極堅剛。

16. 能呼吸。然後能靈活。

17. 氣以直養而無害。勁以曲蓄而有餘。

18. 心為令。氣為旗。腰為纛。

19. 先求開展。後求緊湊。乃可臻於縝密矣。

20. 又曰：「彼不動，己不動。彼微動，己先動。」

21. 勁似鬆非鬆，將展未展。勁斷意不斷。

22. 又曰：「先在心，後在身。」

23. 腹鬆氣沉入骨。神舒體靜。

24. 刻刻在心。切記：一動無有不動，一靜無有不靜。

25. 牽動往來，氣貼背而斂入脊骨。

26. 內固精神。外示安逸

27. 邁步如貓行。運勁如抽絲。

28. 全身意在精神，不在氣；在氣則滯。
    有氣則無力。無氣則純剛。
    氣若車輪，腰如車軸。

13. To receive is to release, if it disconnects then reconnect.

14. In moving forwards and backwards, there should be folding.
    In advancing and retreating, there should be changes of direction.

15. Extreme softness yields to extreme firmness and tenacity.

16. Only with the ability to inhale and exhale, will there be agility.

17. When *qì* is cultivated naturally, there is no harm.
    When the *jìn* (relaxed force) is stored, there will be a surplus.

18. The *xīn* (mind/heart) is the commander, the *qì* is the flag and the *yāo* (waist) is the banner.

19. First seek expansion while opening then seek contraction while closing.
    It will lead to perfect refinement.

20. It is said; "If the other does not move, I do not move.
    If the other has the slightest movement, I move ahead".

21. The *jìn* (force) seems *sōng* (relaxed), however it is not *sōng* (relaxed),
    it is about to expand, although it has not yet expanded.
    The *jìn* (relaxed force) might disconnect, but the mind must not.

22. It is also said: "First the *xīn* (mind/heart), then the body".

23. When the abdomen relaxes, the *qì* sinks into the bones.
    When the *shén* (spirit) calms, the body becomes tranquil.

24. Keep this in *xīn* (in your heart).
    Remember; when you move, every part moves.
    When you settle, every part settles.

25. When moving forwards and backwards,
    the *qì* sticks to the back and permeates into the spine.

26. Internally be acutely aware of the *shén* (spirit),
    externally appear calm and relaxed.

27. Step like a cat.
    Transmit the *jìn* (force) like reeling silk from a cocoon.

28. The *yì* (intention) should be on the *jìngshén* (spirit), not on the *qì*,
    otherwise the *qì* will stagnate.
    With *qì*, extra-ordinary power will develop.
    Without *qì* there will only be *lì* (brute strength).
    Qì is like the cart wheel and the *yāo* (waist) is like the axle.

1. The flow of *qì* is directed by the mind, first into the *dāntián*, then to the limbs and finally through the *huìyīn* meridian point to the three gates the *wěilú*, *yùzhěn* and *níwán*. This enables the *qì* to be absorbed into the bones.

2. If the body has its centre of equilibrium, relaxed and connected, the *qì* will be able to flow unhindered throughout the body. When the *qì* can flow unrestricted, it can be directed by the will of the mind.

3. When the *shén* (spirit) is raised and the *huìyīn* and *níwán* meridian points are in line, the centre of equilibrium is attained. The body will therefore be upright, centred, balanced and not sluggish. This is what is meant by the principle of visualising the head to be suspended from above.

4. When the movement is initiated by the mind leading the *qì*, the mind and *qì* interact with agility. The body is therefore able to move without hindrance, providing that the central equilibrium is maintained, the body is centred and grounded as well as left / right, up / down, being in balance. Then the flow of *qì* will naturally be circular and lively. This is also the meaning of, 'changing the substantiality'.

5. When executing *fājìn* (releasing the relaxed force), the body must be relaxed. Any tension of the body will reduce the percentage of grounding, and undermine the root. Tension will also lessen the connection of the arms to the body, the body to the base, and the base / feet to the ground. If *jìn* (relaxed force) is stored for release but the body is tense, up to 50% will be consumed by your own muscles, leaving a maximum of a half to be transmitted into the opponent. Complete relaxation is the only way to release the entire force, unrestricted.

    Sinking is a mental process in which the mind directs the *qì* downwards through the body into the feet into the ground, creating a root, which is used to "borrow the energy from the earth". Therefore if the body relaxes and sinks, compression develops which produces the spring-like *jìn* (relaxed force). When this *jìn* (relaxed force) is released the mind should focus on the direction and project as far as possible beyond the opponent.

6. While the body is upright, the centre of equilibrium can be attained. When the body is loose, it is relaxed and free of tension. When the mind is tranquil, it can harmonise with the

body. Then by being upright, loose and tranquil together, the upper body can become light and the base heavy (grounded), therefore able to support the body in all eight directions (the four cardinals plus the four diagonals).

7. The original Chinese text translates as "direct the *qì* like threading the nine bend pearls". However it should not be taken literally, the term threading the nine bend pearls refers to flowing continuously. When the *qì* flows continuously, it reaches everywhere smoothly. When the body is centred, relaxed and connected, the mind will be able to direct the *qì* into the *dāntián* continuously, and from the *dāntián* into the feet, from which it rebounds into the fingers.

   When the *qì* is able to flow smoothly and continuously throughout the body, from the *Huìyīn* to the *níwán* (crown of the head), the relaxed force produced is as pure and powerful as tempered steel. When discharged nothing will be able to withstand it.

8. When an eagle is preying on a hare, it circles with sharp eyes alert for any movement. When a cat stalks a mouse, it is calm, relaxed and focused, only pouncing when the time is right. Similarly in *tuīshŏu* (pushing-hands), be sensitive at all times, and seize on every opportunity the moment it arises. The eagle represents staying aware for a chance to attack, while the cat signifies recognising the correct timing and direction. Avoid pushing blindly, when there is no opportunity to warrant it. A poorly timed, or wrongly directed attack will certainly miss.

9. When not moving one should be as calm, still, grounded and sturdy as a mountain. When moving one should be as flowing, soft and powerful as a river washing away everything in its path.

10. Before an arrow can be released, the string of the bow must be drawn to create the elastic force. A spring must be compressed before it can produce a rebounding force. Similarly, before the body's *jìn* (relaxed force) is released, it is necessary to sink and load up. When releasing an arrow from a bow there should not be any hesitation, the same applies to *fājìn* (releasing of the force). Hesitation will reduce the power released.

11. The yielding and neutralising movements are circular. When attacking, if you can establish a line from your feet through the point of contact into the opponent's substantial foot, you can bisect the opponent's circle, and render their neutralisation ineffective.

   Neutralising in curves is *yīn*, attacking in straight lines is *yáng*. Therefore by neutralising without attacking, it is *yīn* without *yáng*, and usually results in being forced into a corner and still being pushed over. Continuing to attack in the one direction without turning, is *yáng* without *yīn*, and most often results in being over-extended and easily rolled-back or plucked out. Therefore in straight there should be a curve and visa versa, then *yīn* and *yáng* will be in harmony.

   Sink to build up the energy, storing it before it is released.

12. When executing *fājìn* (releasing the relaxed force), the *jìn* (relaxed force) is transmitted through the back. During the process of releasing the tail bone tucks under to provide space for the back muscles to relax, the shoulder blades drop downward, and the shoulders sink. The footwork must follow the changes of the body movements.

13. To receive is to accept an incoming force without any resistance, allowing it to pass through the body into the ground, thereby completely neutralising it. It is not simply a sequence of entirely neutralising the incoming force then releasing your own, *yīn* and *yáng* must always be in harmony. This means that if there is ten percent of neutralising ten percent of force should be already returning to the attacker. This is very clearly demonstrated at the stage of *jiējìn* (receiving force). Whenever there is disconnection, connection must be restored immediately.

14. When moving forwards or backwards the technique of folding should be used. So that if the palm is neutralised, the forearm follows in, by folding at the wrist. Similarly if the forearm is neutralised the elbow folds for the upper arm to follow in, and if the upper arm is neutralised, the shoulder folds for the body to follow in. This is also what is meant by the statement; "the hands are not [the only] hands, the whole body is a hand". When advancing or retreating there must always be a change in direction to avoid moving in a straight line.

15. Extreme softness does not mean becoming limp or floppy. Rather it means to relax and let go of unnecessary physical tension while maintaining the body's structure. This will produce a spring like resilience.

16. Breathing naturally without holding the breath or panting, enables the body to relax and become agile.

17. When *qì* is cultivated and circulated, it results in good health, benefiting not harming the body. By storing the *jìn* (relaxed force) it becomes readily available. Continuously relaxing, sinking, and connecting, provides an ongoing supply of *jìn* (relaxed force). In *tàijí*, when such a force is constantly present in the body, it is termed *péngjìn*.

18. The *xīn* (mind/heart) directs the *qì*, therefore the *qì* follows the direction of the mind and motivates the body. The *yāo* (waist) controls the direction of the movement.

19. In the beginning the movements should be practised big and expansive to open the joints and stretch the ligaments. As the practitioner progresses, the timing refines, and the posture sequences connect. These refinements naturally result in the movements becoming smaller more compact, and synchronised.

20. The movements of *tuīshǒu* (pushing-hands) should be initiated by your opponent. Therefore if your partner does not move, you do not move. By synchronising with his or her slightest movement and remaining connected, you can lead them into over committing themselves. This is what is meant by "moving ahead", and is a clear example of *dǒngjìn* (understanding of the forces).

21. The *jìn* (relaxed force) is neither hard nor soft, rather it is firm and springy. Every expansion also requires contraction, and in the *fājìn* (releasing of the force) there must be sinking.

    After discharging your opponent, your *jìn* disconnects but your mind's focus should continue to project in the same direction.

22. If the *xīn* (mind/heart) is made king and the body the subject, the mind can command and the body will follow.

23. When the abdomen is relaxed the *qì* will sink into the *dāntián*. From the *dāntián* it flows throughout the body and into the bones, increasing the density of the bone marrow.

    When the *shén* (spirit) is calm and in harmony with the mind, the body will be relaxed.

24. To begin any posture, every part of the body connects and changes to create the movement. To complete a posture every part of the body synchronises, so that even though they have different destinations, their time of arrival will be the same. In *tuīshǒu* (pushing-hands) when your opponents' force is on you, it is the whole body that adjusts, not just the area immediately around the contact points.

25. When the *qì* is able to pass through the *huìyīn* meridian point to the *níwán* (crown of the head) meridian point, it indicates being in the third stage of the Earth level. At this point, when the *qì* travels through the three gates it will permeate into the spine and other bones.

26. Internally the mind and *shén* (spirit) must be calm, and externally there must not be any tension, for the *qì* to flow unhindered.

27. The footwork should be soft and balanced yet stable and grounded, just like a cat walking. During releasing, the *jìn* (relaxed force) should be one continuous flow, from the feet through the legs, hips, body, arms and fingers, without any pause or break. Just like reeling off the silk from a cocoon.

28. The *yì* (mind intention) should be on the *jìngshén* (spirit), not on the *qì*. If you are thinking of the *qì*, your thoughts are locked in your head and your awareness has not travelled into the body. Therefore the *qì* can't flow and may stagnate. Movements containing flowing *qì*, will eventually develop extra-ordinary power (mental force). Movements absent of flowing *qì*, will only acquire *lì* (brute strength). The waist as the axle, controls the horizontal (left and right) direction of the revolving *qì*.

打手歌

1. 掤攦擠按須認真。

2. 上下相隨人難進。

3. 任他巨力來打吾。

4. 牽動四兩撥千斤。

5. 引進落空合即出。

6. 黏連貼隨不丟頂。

1. Be diligent about *péng* (ward-off), *lǚ* (roll-back),
    jǐ (press) and *àn* (push).

2. [If] Upper and lower are sychronised,
    it will be difficult for the other to come in.

3. Let him use immense *lì* (brute strength) to hit me.

4. Lead his movements with only four *tael* (approx. 15 grams) to neutralise a thousand *catty*
    (approx. 240 grams) of force.

5. Draw him into emptiness, join, gather [the force] then send it out.

6. *Nián* (adhere), *lián* (connect), *tiē* (stick), [and] *suí* (follow),
    without disconnecting or resisting.

1. Being diligent is to not take it lightly, it is to study carefully and seriously. *Péng* (ward-off), *lǚ* (roll-back), *jǐ* (press) and *àn* (push) are the four cardinal directions in *tuīshǒu* (pushing-hands), attention must be paid to the accuracy of practising them. The practitioners should recognise when to *àn* (push); when to *lǚ* (roll-back); when to *jǐ* (press); and when to *péng* (ward-off). When using *lǚ*, you should not roll-back on to your own body. When using *péng*, you should not ward off on to the opponent's body. When *àn* (pushing) or *jǐ* (pressing), you should store the energy (absorb or sink) before releasing it. It is important to pay attention to the timing of yielding and neutralising.

2. The upper and lower body must be connected, centred and aligned. Every part of the body is sychronised and moves in relation to each other, therefore making it difficult for an opponent to find a gap to enter and attack.

3. Let the opponent expend all his force and effort attacking.

4. Even if your opponent attacks with a lot of strength (one thousand *catty*), by following the direction and the momentum without resisting, the attack has nothing to land on. It then only requires a very small amount (four *tael*) of force to deflect and neutralise the opponent's attack.

    Note: *Tael* and *catty* are ancient Chinese units to measure weight. 16 *taels* equal one *catty* (one *tael* is equals approximately 15 grams, one *catty* equals approximately 240 grams).

5. By yielding in the direction of attacking forces and following the momentum without resisting, you can extend your attackers' force to the point of them losing their balance, falling into emptiness. Meanwhile by connecting into your own root, you develop your own force, so when your opponents realise that they are out of their centre, you can stick to their withdrawal and release the energy that you have stored.

6. You should be like a sponge, which goes in as much as it is pushed and comes back as much as the withdraw. When you can *tiē* (stick), *lián* (connect), *nián* (adhere), [and] *suí* (follow), without disconnecting or resisting, you will be able to follow any changes that the opponent makes. Practising all these qualities develops *tīngjìn* (listening energy) *dǒngjìn* (understanding energy) and ultimately *shénmíng* (spiritual clarity / enlightenment).

楊家太極拳要領
　　　楊澄莆口授

1. 虛靈頂勁。

2. 含胸拔背。

3. 鬆腰。

4. 分虛實。

5. 沉肩墜肘。

6. 用意不用力。

7. 上下相隨。

8. 內外相合。

9. 相連不斷。

10. 動中求靜。

11. 似拉鋸式。

12. 我不是肉架子。

13. 磨轉心不轉。

14. 撥不倒，不倒翁。

Tàijí Classic (vi): **Important Tàijí points from the Yang Family**

— *Yang Cheng-Fu*

1.   Raise the *shén* (spirit) to the crown of the head.

2.   *Hán* (contain - not reveal) the chest and *bá* (spread) the back.

3.   *Sōng* (relax) the *yāo* (waist).

4.   Differentiate *shí* (substantial) from *xū* (insubstantial).

5.   *Chén* (sink) the shoulders and hang [drop] the elbows

6.   Use *yì* (mind intention) not *lì* (brute strength).

7.   Upper and lower body synchronise.

8.   Internal and external are in harmony.

9.   Be connected, without discontinuity.

10.   Seek calmness in movement.

11.   [Be like] two men sawing.

12.   I'm not a meat rack.

13.   The millstone turns but the axle does not [turn].

14.   Be an upright doll that cannot be pushed over.

Discussion on: *Important Tàijí points from the Yang family*

1. Raising the *shén* (spirit) to the crown of the head is the same concept as holding the head as though being suspended from above, and being conscious of the crown of the head. When I began training directly under *Huang Sheng-Shyan*, he occasionally placed an empty matchbox on my head while I practised, which assisted me to maintain an awareness of the crown of my head throughout the form. Subsequently the body became upright with the *níwán* and the *huìyīn* meridians points aligned. After achieving that, the postures revolve around the centre of equilibrium, which ensures agility in all the body movements.

2. *Hán* (contain not reveal) the chest by relaxing and emptying the chest from within. To avoid hunching the back while doing this, visualise the crown of the head as being suspended from above.

   To *bá* (spread) the back, remove all tension in the back muscles and allow the shoulder blades to drop downwards. The *qì* will only sink into the *dāntián* when the chest is relaxed and emptied and the back is spread.

3. Relax the *yāo* (waist) by letting go of tension around the torso's mid section and seat the *kuà* (hips joints) into their sockets. When the *yāo* (waist) relaxes and the *kuà* (hips joints) are seated, there is an increase of mobility in the upper body. Bear in mind in *tàijí*, when the *yāo* (waist) is referred to, it includes operating in conjunction with the *kuà* (hips joints), turning as one.

4. Many *tàijí* practitioners oversimplify the differentiation of substantial from insubstantial, by only distinguishing the distribution of weight. It has more to do with recognising and allocating greater and lesser forces, both incoming and outgoing, and has little to do with positioning body mass over one or the other foot. It is necessary to be able to sink into, and source a force from, both a foot bearing the most and least weight, eventually even at the same time.

   Understanding your own substantiality and insubstantiality includes the principle of cross-alignment (discussed further in my [note 9] interpretation of *Chang San-Feng* classic): When releasing *jìn* (relaxed force) from the right substantial foot, it should be transmitted through the left substantial arm and vice-versa. This what is meant by "when the right is substantial the right is insubstantial and when the left is substantial the left is insubstantial". The ability to harmonise and change with any situation can only be achieved when able to differentiate the substantial from the insubstantial forces.

5. To *chén* (sink) the shoulders, is to soften the area around the shoulder joints and let go of the shoulder blades, with a downward intention. This connects the arms with the body. Hanging the elbows is achieved by letting the weight of the arms drop them downward, but not to a point of collapsing. In *tuīshǒu* (pushing-hands) the sinking of the shoulders allows the *jìn* (relaxed force) to pass from the torso into the arms, while the hanging of the elbows functions as a pivot, directing the *jìn* (relaxed force) into the feet of the opponent to break the root. The inability to either *chén* (sink) the shoulders or hang the elbows, affects the relaxing and emptying of the chest and spreading of the back, which in turn restricts the sinking of the *qì* into the *dāntián*.

6. Use *yì* (the mind) not *lì* (brute strength). In external martial arts the training is often based around techniques using muscular strength and brute force. Such practice can only lead to the development of *lì* or physical power. *Tàijí* develops an internal power not requiring physical strength, by training the movements to be initiated by the *yì* (mind). The *yì* (mind) directs the *qì*, the *qì* motivates the physical movement. When the *qì* reaches maximum compression, the *jìn* (relaxed force) produced becomes an internal power.

7. To achieve upper and lower body synchronisation, an understanding is required of the sequence of changes that create the movement. The sequences are timed to change in relation to one another, as connected movements not just co-ordinated actions. When you move, every part of the body should be moving, and when the movement settles, every part should come to rest.

8. For the internal and external to be in harmony, whenever the mind has an opening intention, the physical movement must also open. Conversely whenever the mind has a closing intention, the physical movement must also close.

9. In the *tàijí* form, from beginning to end the movements are a continuous flow without disconnection. Like the rolling flow of the river, that never ends and leaves no gap for an opponent to enter. The *qì* is also a continuous flow, circulating like the currents of the ocean, with the *jìn* (relaxed force) as the constantly recurring waves.

10. When physically moving in *tàijí*, the mind must remain calm and attentive. Calmness can only be achieved when the focus is brought within. In the *tàijí* form, calmness of the mind cultivates awareness of the changes throughout the movements. While during *tuīshǒu* (pushing-hands), calmness enables better detection of the opponent's intention.

11. Visualise two men using a two-person saw. Working in harmony they utilise the principles of sticking, adhering, following, while not resisting or disconnecting.

12. A meat rack is a place to hang dead flesh. During *tuīshǒu* (pushing-hands), don't lean on your opponent, or use insensitive heavy hands. Stick using the lightest touch necessary to connect to his or her base. You are not a meat rack either; don't allow any force to build up on you.

13. Visualise a line running centrally through the body from the *níwán* (crown of the head) connecting to the *huìyīn* meridian point. This serves as the body's axle (central axis). Wherever a millstone is located, it still moves by rotating around its axle. Like the millstone, the body position can change but it should revolve around the central axis. To function effectively the millstone must remain level and the axle vertical, similarly the body's central axis should be kept upright particularly while turning. The centre of equilibrium can be easily maintained, when turning like a millstone.

14. Be like a self-righting doll, which being weighted at the bottom and light on top, cannot be pushed over. Visualise the crown of the head as being suspended from above, so that the spine is straight and the body vertical, and the centre of equilibrium can be maintained at all times. The feet must be firmly grounded, the upper body relaxed, the mind calm with continuous waves of *chén* (sinking) deep into the earth, even while an external force is affecting you. When this is achieved the upper body will be relaxed and light, the base will be grounded and heavy, like the self-righting doll.

體用歌

1. 太極拳，十三式。
   妙在二氣分陰陽。

2. 化生千億歸抱一。
   歸抱一，太極拳。

3. 兩儀四象渾無邊，
   禦風何似頂頭懸。

4. 我有一轉語，今為知者吐：
   「湧泉無根腰無主，力學垂死終無補。」

5. 體用相兼豈有他。
   浩然氣能行乎手。

6. 掤攦擠按採挒肘靠進退顧盼定。

7. 不化自化走自走。
   足欲向前先挫後。

8. 身似行雲，打手安用手。
   渾身是手手非手。

9. 但須方寸隨時守所守。

1. *Tàijíquán*, - the thirteen postures.
   The marvel lies in the nature of *qì*; *yīn* and yáng.

2. It changes into infinity and returns to the one.
   Returns to the one, *tàijíquán*.

3. The two primary principles (*yīn* and *yáng*)
   and four manifestations are without boundary.

   To ride the wind, the head is suspended at the crown, from above.

4. I have words for those who can understand:
   "If the *yǒngquán* (bubbling well) has no root, or the *yāo* (waist) has no control, life long practice will be in vain".

5. There is no secret about the substance and function, they interrelate.
   The only way is to let the wide and flowing *qì* extend into the fingers.

6. Always remain in central equilibrium during *péng* (ward-off), *lǚ* (roll-back), *jǐ* (press), *àn* (push), *cǎi* (pluck), *liè* (split), *zhǒu* (elbow-strike) and *kào* (lean-on), and also when stepping forward, sitting backward, looking left, looking right, and staying centred.

7. Neutralising without neutralising, yielding without yielding.
   Sit back before you move forward.

8. When the body is like a cloud, the whole body functions as the hands.
   The hands are not the [only] hands.

9. The mind must always remain aware.

Discussion on: **The Song of Substance and Function**

1. *Tàijíquán* consists of the original thirteen postures: *Péng* (ward-off), *lǚ* (roll-back), *jǐ* (press), and *àn* (push) as the four cardinal directions, *cǎi* (pluck), *liè* (split), *zhǒu* (elbow-strike) and *kào* (lean-on) being the four oblique angles. Plus the five elements of stepping forward, sitting back, looking left, looking right, staying centred. The amazing thing about *tàijíquán* is that it is never ending, constantly interacting, changing between *yīn* and *yáng*.

2. It is capable of an endless number of changes and yet able to harmonise and unify into one, that is *tàijíquán*.

3. The changes of *yīn* and *yáng* and four manifestations are not limited by space or time.

   Riding the wind means to be able to adapt to unpredictable changes in the situation and the force. To be able to ride the wind you must have an aligned centre of equilibrium. When the head is held as though the crown is suspended from the above the *níwán* and *huìyīn* meridian points will be vertically in line, the body will be upright, and therefore the centre of equilibrium will be achieved.

4. The author has words of advice for practitioners wanting to understand *tàijíquán*: The *yǒngquán* (bubbling well) is a meridian point under both feet and serves as the root of the body's posture. It is through these, that both an incoming force is emptied into the earth, and the energy from the earth is passed from the ground into the body. When the *yǒngquán* (bubbling well) in the feet is not connected to the ground, the body is without root and any incoming force will only remain in the body. The result is double heaviness, which hinders the body movement causing inflexibility. The loss of mobility in the hips means that the waist will be unable to control the direction of release. Under these circumstances, even after a lifetime of dedicated practice, no significant benefits will result.

5. There is no secret in the 'substance and function of *tàijíquán*', all is revealed once you are able to guide the *qì* to flow all the way back from the ground into the fingertips. Getting the *qì* to flow to the fingertips is the second stage of training the earth level of *tàijí*. To initiate *fājìn* (releasing of the relaxed force), gather the *qì* into the *dāntián*, then use mind awareness to direct the *qì* from the *dāntián* through the legs into the ground under both feet. Once that is achieved you must again use mind awareness to visualise the *qì* rebounding from the ground under both feet through the legs, up the body, down the arms and into the finger tips.

6. Establishing the centre of equilibrium is the function of the thirteen postures. In the postures of *péng* (ward-off), *lǚ* (roll-back), *jǐ* (press), *àn* (push), *cǎi* (pluck), *liè* (split), *zhǒu* (elbow-strike) and *kào* (lean-on), and also when stepping forward, sitting backward, looking left, looking right, and staying centred, the centre of equilibrium must be maintained.

7. Being able to neutralise without neutralising and yield without yielding is termed *jiējìn* (receiving a force). When a *tàijí* practitioner reaches this high level he or she can change without apparently changing, and act without any apparent action.

   Before moving forward, you should sit back and sink into the rear foot to connect with the root, and if required to free the front foot to step.

8. We can all see a cloud and yet an aircraft passes through without obstruction and cannot land on it. Similarly any incoming force will be unable to find any resistance to utilise if you have established a centre of equilibrium and are *chén* (sinking) so that the base is balanced and grounded, the upper body is centred and completely *sōng* (relaxed). At that stage the neutralising and issuing of the force is not restricted to the arms and hands. Any part of the body can neutralise an incoming force, and every part could be used to *fājìn* (issue the relaxed force). This is what is meant by "The hands are not the hands, the whole body functions as the hands".

9. Mind awareness must be present in every part of the body at all times, and not drift off into thoughts outside of your *tàijí* practice.

àn	(按):	push, forth movement of the grasp the sparrow's tail sequence
bá	(拔):	spread
bǎihuì	(百會):	crown meridian point usually referred to as *níwán* ,
		literal translation: hundred convergences
cǎi	(採):	pluck
chángquán	(長拳):	long fist - early name for *tàijíquán*
chén	(沉):	sink
dāntián	(丹田):	abdominal meridian point, 3cm below navel,
		literal translation: centre of elixir
dàlù	(大路):	first moving step pushing-hands routine, literal meaning: big path
dǒngjìn	(懂勁):	understanding energy
duì	(兌):	western trigram, element: swamp or lake
fājìn	(發勁):	discharge/release relaxed force
fàngsōng	(放鬆):	let go / release
gēn	(根):	base / joints
hán	(含):	contain - not reveal
hū	(呼):	breathe
huìyīn	(會陰):	perineum meridian point between anus and scrotum/vulva,
		literal translation: meeting of *yīn*
jí	(極):	ultimate
jǐ	(擠):	press, third movement of the grasp the sparrow's tail sequence
jiējìn	(接勁):	receiving energy
jìn	(勁):	relaxed force
jīng	(精):	essence
jīnglù	(精路):	meridians, energy pathways
kǎn	(坎):	northern trigram, element: water
kào	(靠):	lean-on
kuà	(胯):	hips
kūn	(坤):	southwestern trigram, element: earth
láogōng	(勞宮):	palm meridian point where third finger touches when hand clenched,
		literal translation: work palace
lí	(離):	southern trigram, element: fire
lí	(厘):	Chinese 'Old System' unit of measurement, a *lí* approximates to 576m
		and thousandth part of a *tael*

lì	(力):	brute strength
lián	(連):	connect
liè	(挒):	split
lǔ	(擺):	roll-back, second movement of the grasp the sparrow's tail sequence
mìngmén	(命門):	lower spine meridian point between 2nd and 3rd lumbar vertebrae, literal translation: life entrance
nián	(黏):	adhere
níwán	(泥丸):	crown of head meridian point sometimes referred to as *bǎihuì*, literal translation: mud pill
péng	(掤):	ward-off, first movement of the grasp the sparrow's tail sequence
qì	(氣):	energy, vigour
quán	(拳):	fist / boxing
qián	(乾):	northwestern trigram, element: heaven
rén	(人):	front mid-line meridian, literal translation: person / man
shén	(神):	spirit
shénmíng	(神明):	enlightenment / spiritual clarity
shuāngzhòng	(雙重):	equal heaviness
sǐ	(死):	dead
shí	(實):	substantial/full
suí	(隨):	follow
tàijíquán	(太極拳):	grand ultimate boxing
tiē	(貼):	stick
tīngjìn	(聽經):	listening energy
tuīshǒu	(推手):	pushing-hands
wěilú	(尾閭):	coccyx meridian point, literal translation: tail gate
wúwéi	(無偽):	non action / natural process
xiǎolù	(小路):	second moving step pushing-hands routine, literal translation: small path
xīn	(心):	heart/conscience
xū	(虛):	insubstantial/empty
xùn	(巽):	southeastern trigram, element: wind
yāo	(腰):	waist
yáng	(陽):	male principle: expansive
yì	(意):	mind intention
yīn	(陰):	female principle: recessive
yǒngquán	(湧泉):	sole meridian point, in depression between pads of 2nd and 3rd toes, literal translation: bubbling well
yùzhěn	(玉枕):	occipital meridian point, literal translation: jade pillow
zhèn	(震):	eastern trigram, element: thunder
zhōngzhèng	(中正):	central equilibrium
zhǒu	(肘):	elbow-strike